The Westwood Tarot

Yasmeen Westwood
Written by **KALLIOPE**

Copyright © 2024, illustrated by Yasmeen Westwood,
written by Kalliope Haratsidis

Library of Congress Control Number: 2024932130

All rights reserved. No part of this work may be
reproduced or used in any form or by any means—
graphic, electronic, or mechanical, including
photocopying or information storage and retrieval
systems—without written permission from the
publisher.

The scanning, uploading, and distribution of this book
or any part thereof via the Internet or any other means
without the permission of the publisher is illegal and
punishable by law. Please purchase only authorized
editions and do not participate in or encourage the
electronic piracy of copyrighted materials.

"Red Feather Mind Body Spirit" logo is a trademark
of Schiffer Publishing, Ltd.
"Red Feather Mind Body Spirit Feather" logo is a
registered trademark of Schiffer Publishing, Ltd.

Cover design by Danielle Farmer
Designed by BMac
Type set in Juice/Minion

ISBN: 978-0-7643-6812-7
Printed in China

Published by REDFeather Mind, Body, Spirit
An imprint of Schiffer Publishing, Ltd.
4880 Lower Valley Road
Atglen, PA 19310
Phone: (610) 593-1777; Fax: (610) 593-2002
Email: Info@redfeathermbs.com
Web: www.redfeathermbs.com

For Arran Kane Westwood . . .
the wee tall majestic warrior of the West Woods . . .
YW

To my father, Kosta,
who believed me when I told him about my little green
man. Thanks, Dad, for always believing in me;
this one's for you.
KH

Contents

WELCOME 5

THE CREATION OF *The Westwood Tarot* 6

PATHWAYS OF EMPOWERMENT 7

DIVINING THE CARDS 8

THE SUITS 9

THE COURTS 10

THE MAJOR ARCANA 12

THE MINOR ARCANA 82

SPREADS 252

AUTHOR BIOS 256

Each player must accept the cards life deals him or her;
but once they are in hand, he or she alone must decide how to
play the cards in order to win the game.

Voltaire

Welcome

Welcome to the enchanting world of *The Westwood Tarot*, where you will embark on a transformative journey guided by captivating characters and the mystical allure of ancient woods. As you explore this guidebook, prepare to immerse yourself in a sense of calm where words dance and symbols speak directly to your soul, unveiling hidden truths and stirring your deepest emotions. *The Westwood Tarot* beckons you to delve into the depths of your subconscious, where profound insights and revelation await. Inspired by pure intuition and decades of experience, this deck is a testament to the innate connections among artistry, intuition, and profound human experiences. Each card is a gateway to a rich tapestry of stories, carrying the wisdom of ages and offering intuitive guidance that resonates with the very essence of your being. Within these pages, you will encounter a cast of unforgettable characters who have stepped forth from fantastical realms to share their unique perspectives and stories. They will serve as your trusted allies, providing deep wisdom and intuitive guidance to help you find answers, ignite your creativity, and embrace the power within.

The Westwood Tarot is not merely a divination tool; it's a catalyst for personal growth, transformation, and self-discovery. This guidebook is a treasure trove of insights, offering comprehensive interpretations of each card's light and shadow aspects. As you navigate their stories, you will navigate your own, uncovering new paths, exploring probable outcomes, and finding space and inspiration along the way. It is an invitation to connect with your subconscious mind, to feel the raw intensity of your emotions, and to uncover the mysteries that lie beneath the surface. *The Westwood Tarot* is a culmination of a lifelong journey, a testament to the profound connections among the human experience, intuition, magick of divination, and the natural world around us. It is a tool that evolves with you, deepening your understanding of its mysticism and empowering you to navigate the complexities of life with clarity and purpose.

So, with open hearts and minds, let us embark on this extraordinary Fool's Journey together. Let *The Westwood Tarot* be your guide as you unlock the secrets to the universe and discover the transformative power within. For throughout these pages lies the key to a world where stories cannot be told; they must be discovered. We welcome you to *The Westwood Tarot*, where the pages of this guidebook become doorways and where magick and wisdom intertwine to illuminate the depths of your soul and awaken your truest potential.

With abundant love and boundless magick,
Intriguingly yours,
Kalliope & Yasmeen

The important thing is not to stop questioning.
Curiosity has its own reason for existing. One cannot help
but be in awe when he contemplates the mysteries of eternity,
of life, of the marvelous structure of reality.
It is enough if one tries merely to comprehend a little of this mystery
every day. Never lose a holy curiosity.

Albert Einstein

The Creation of
The Westwood Tarot

In the creation of *The Westwood Tarot*, Yasmeen draws upon her cherished childhood memories spent immersed in the enchanted world of *The Magic Faraway Tree* by Enid Blyton. Inspired by the limitless realms of imagination, the deck's imagery springs forth, transporting us to a magickal land filled with weird and wonderful characters, where there are no rules and anything goes. Through her artistic vision, Yasmeen invites us to explore this whimsical tapestry of magic, woven into the cards, where the boundaries of imagination are limitless and the extraordinary awaits.

Pathways of Empowerment

Embrace the Keys to Divine Connection

Step into the realm of transformative readings, crafting a sacred sanctuary within your space. Set the ambiance with flickering candles, melodies that soothe the soul, coupled with a heartfelt intention. Welcome the magick that reveals profound insights and mystical connections and stirs your intuition. Enter a world where images whisper, and the ordinary transmutes into the extraordinary.

Before you begin a reading, review the Five Cs below.

THE FIVE CS

CENTER Focus your energy with three intentional breaths, inhaling through your nose and exhaling out your mouth, bringing inner balance and presence.

CLEAR Visualize a shimmering ball of golden-white light at your feet. Slowly guide this radiant energy upward through your body, from the soles of your feet to the crown of your head. See it cascade around your body, creating a protective bubble around your aura.

CONNECT Turn your focus to the center of your being and merge with the divine spark within, as you embrace the infinite wisdom and guidance of the universe. Experience profound connection and divine alignment.

CALL Invoke your Higher Self, trusted animal and spirit guides, elemental beings, and divine helpers, whom you have a personal connection with, asking for their presence, guidance, and protection.

CLOSE After completion of the reading, express gratitude to your guides. Shuffle and store the cards. Take three deep cleansing breaths. Visualize radiant sunlight above your head; bring it down through your body, connecting the energy with Mother Earth's core through the soles of your feet. Feel the grounding energy as you close the session.

Divining the Cards

In this guidebook, you'll find that each card description contains the following.

MNEMONIC Embrace the power of poetic mnemonics to grasp the card's energy, attitude, and keywords. It is a valuable tool for understanding each card's essence.

IMAGE The captivating imagery and symbolism of the card awaken your intuition. Let your spirit visually connect and absorb the wisdom of the arcana.

KEYWORDS Reveal both the Light and Shadow aspects, embracing both positive and negative qualities. The key is to discover magick of balance, for within every card lies shades of gray. If you read reversals, look to the Shadow for your answer.

SCENE In this unconventional deck, Scenes replace descriptions. Let them unfold before your eyes, guiding your intuition as you get a glimpse into their world.

CATEGORIES Each card offers a tailored message for specific areas of life, including love, career, wellness, and finances. Find special guidance in the category you seek.

MAGICK—WISDOM—FURTHER INDULGENCE Discover the Magick and Wisdom within each card, with the 22 Majors offering Further Indulgence. Experience the magick of all the cards, as they offer insightful nuggets of wisdom along the way.

SPIRIT GUIDES Embark on your journey with a wise guide by your side, illustrated in each card, as you navigate *The Westwood Tarot*.

QUOTES Thoughtfully selected quotes enhancing the energetic significance of each card.

FINAL THOUGHTS

The Westwood Tarot is a deck suitable for all experience levels, offering unique opportunities for each level of reader. Beginners will be enthralled with the soft and whimsical images, while establishing a solid foundation with the 78 cards. Experienced practitioners will discover new concepts and perspectives, inviting them to delve into the nuances of each card. For professionals, this deck presents thought-provoking insights to enhance their craft, while guiding clients to explore the depths of their shadows. Regardless of your skill level, consistent practice is key to mastering the Tarot.

The Suits

There are four suits that make up the Minor Arcana: Wands, Cups, Swords, and Pentacles. They are the equivalent of the Clubs, Hearts, Spades, and Diamonds in a deck of playing cards.

The numerological order of the Tarot would be Ace through 10, followed by the Courts, which comprise Pages, Knights, Queens, and Kings. This makes a total of 56 cards for the Minor Arcana. Let's introduce the suits of the Minor Arcana.

THE SUIT OF WANDS

The suit of Wands begins with the season of spring, where new life buds. The tiny spark from the Wands ignites beginnings with the element of fire and directional south.

THE SUIT OF CUPS

As the season turns into the fullness of those hot, lazy days of summer, Cups, brimming with the element of water, represent directional west.

THE SUIT OF SWORDS

Leading into the harvest of autumn, the airy Swords cut through, representing directional east.

THE SUIT OF PENTACLES

As with all things, in the winter of life all things must return to the earth, symbolized by the Pentacle and representing directional north.

The Courts

In *The Westwood Tarot*, the Court cards are seen as representations of individuals. In my practice, I have assigned astrological signs to each royal, offering a valuable perspective into their unique qualities. The exception is the Knights, since they primarily symbolize timing, speed, and movement.

The Court cards could represent someone you know with similar traits, while also revealing aspects of your own character. Understanding the Courts can be challenging, but I remember each royal by associating them with individuals or movie characters that fit their script. By observing their interactions, imagining their conversations, and observing their mannerisms and words, you can unravel the enigma of the Courts.

THE ROYAL COURT OF WANDS

This Court embodies the passionate Fire signs of the zodiac. They begin with the Page of Wands, a bold and adventurous Aries, followed by the Queen of Wands, a charismatic and creative Leo, and concluding with the King of Wands, a visionary and confident Sagittarius. Together, they share common traits of passion, enthusiasm, and leadership. However, they may also exhibit tendencies toward impulsiveness, arrogance, and a fiery temperament. These Fire signs are trailblazers, inspiring others with their magnetic presence and infectious energy.

THE ROYAL COURT OF CUPS

This Court embodies the sensitive and intuitive nature of the Water signs of the zodiac. They begin with the Page of Cups, a romantic and imaginative Pisces, followed by the Queen of Cups, an empathetic and nurturing Cancer, and concluding with the King of Cups, an intuitive and compassionate Scorpio. Together, they share common traits of emotional depth, sensitivity, and intuition. However, they may also experience moodiness, emotional vulnerability, and a tendency to retreat into their inner worlds. These Water signs offer profound empathy and are deeply connected to the emotions of others.

THE ROYAL COURT OF SWORDS

This Court embodies the intellectual and communicative Air signs of the zodiac. They begin with the Page of Swords, a quick-thinking and assertive Gemini, followed by the Queen of Swords, a wise and analytical Libra, and concluding with the King of Swords, a logical and strategic Aquarius. Together, they share common traits of intellect, objectivity, and eloquence. However, they may also exhibit tendencies toward vengeance, mental detachment, and sharp tongues. These Air signs excel in rational thinking, problem-solving, and articulating their ideas with "pointed" precision.

THE ROYAL COURT OF PENTACLES

This Court embodies the grounded and practical Earth signs of the zodiac. They start with the Page of Pentacles, a diligent and reliable Taurus, followed by the Queen of Pentacles, a nurturing and abundant Virgo, and concluding with the King of Pentacles, a prosperous and dependable Capricorn. Together, they share common traits of stability, practicality, and a strong work ethic. However, they may also be prone to stubbornness, materialism, and a focus on security. These Earth signs excel in manifesting their goals, creating financial abundance, and nurturing a stable foundation.

The Major Arcana

The Fool's journey begins at the symbolic 0, representing the soul's path to enlightenment. As the Fool travels through the Major Arcana, profound archetypes cross her path, revealing esoteric wisdoms. Each card encountered unravels the intricacies of her incarnation, unveiling karmic influences and imparting essential life lessons toward the end of the Major Arcana, where we find the World. Finally, at world's end, the Fool attains self-actualization, grateful for the opportunity to embrace life's splendors.

0 The Fool

*Embarking on the Fool's journey,
from the realm of naught astray
Through life's tapestry I wander,
meeting guides along the way
With a youthful traveling spirit,
chasing bliss with an open heart
My humanity entwines in a spiral
dance, bringing a fresh start*

KEYWORDS & CONCEPTS

LIGHT: innocence, fresh start, naiveté, carefree, leap of faith, spontaneous, playful, adventure, merry, free spirit, traveler, exploring, humanity, enthusiastic, awe, Fool's journey, bliss, initiate, potential, spiritedness, escapades, laughter

SHADOW: childish, nomadic, ignorance, foolishness, immature, oblivious, irresponsible, caution, impetuous, clueless, foolhardy, ignoring advice, learning lessons, missing the signs, careless, ignoring guides, wrong way, unaware, Fool's errand

Scene As the Grasshopper stood on the precipice, going down the steps that led to her grand adventure, she tightly clutched her fuchsia-colored purse, ensuring she had the security of all her worldly possessions for the journey. The vibrant hue of her purse matched her spirit, a symbol of fun and determination to embrace her fresh start. Adorning her head is a hat, exploding with a profuse abundance of purple flowers, as a reminder of her innate gifts and a gentle nudge to pause and appreciate the beauty of life along the way. The sweet fragrance of the wildflowers hung in the air, as if nature itself was rejoicing in her presence. With each exploratory step she descended, the

Grasshopper felt the weight of anticipation and excitement growing within her. The World eagerly awaited her arrival as she prepared to take a daring leap of faith, on an odyssey that would shape her very existence. As she hopped from one step to the next, her heart danced with a mix of nervousness and exhalation. Mischievous orbs provoked her with their antics, in the hopes of instilling fear and diverting her from the stony path. Their shouts echoed the voice of her incarnation's darkness: "You Fool, wrong way!" Unperturbed by the resounding cries, the Fool paid no heed, refusing to waver from her soul's desired experiences. Throwing caution to the wind, she naively takes the next exploratory step, trusting in things she cannot yet see. But feeling better prepared with an umbrella protecting her body from unwanted energies and looking toward the World through her rose-tinted eyes, she'll begin to see life anew.

As she continued on her descent, the butterflies flitted alongside her, their delicate wings mirroring her own sense of freedom and metamorphosis. They guide her through the labyrinth of steps, their presence comforting and reassuring. With each hop, the Grasshopper felt the world shift around her, a kaleidoscope of colors and emotions exploding in front of her eyes, and in her being. The journey was not just about reaching the end but reveling in the present, savoring the moment of this newfound freedom. Basking in the sunshine of her life, she tilted her head to feel the warmth of the sun on her face, relishing the touch of the breeze that ruffled her umbrella. With every leap she shed layers of doubt and naiveté, growing more confident in her ability to navigate the unknown. Her butterfly guides sing enchanting melodies, encouraging her to follow her instincts and trust the path unfolding before her. The Grasshopper, in all her grace and audacity, knows that this journey would be a testament to her resolve and resilience. With a merry heart filled with adventure, the Grasshopper hopped onto each step, propelling her closer to the grand finale and into the waiting arms of the World.

Fool in Love Take a leap into love, embracing spontaneity, and venture into unexplored relationships. Don those rose-tinted eyes and allow yourself to be footloose and fancy-free in your pursuit of love. If already in a relationship, rediscover the joy and excitement of your early days together.

Fool in Career There is a time and place for everything. It might be admirable to lighten the mood of the workplace by embracing your inner joker, but it is a sure way to keep you stuck in the same role. Think about it: Who willingly entrusts the keys to the kingdom to a Fool? A Fool!

Fool in Wellness Laughter is the ultimate medicine for well-being, so don't hesitate to laugh at yourself once in a while. It brings a sense of lightness to a too-serious world. However, be cautious when using the phrase "Just joking" to communicate real feelings, or a nervous laugh to mask genuine emotions.

Fool in Finances Embrace risks, reap the reward, and have some skin in the game. Freedom comes in discerning when to leap and when to wait. See through financial illusions; remove the rose-tinted glasses when looking at financial matters. Dare to think differently; success awaits the strange and bold.

The Magick of the Fool As a wild spirit, the Fool dances to the beat of their own drum, unbound by conventional constraints. Follow your heart's desire, trusting your guides to take you to places you were destined to explore. An exhilarating adventure awaits, so embrace the thrill of the unknown, welcoming it with open arms instead of letting it paralyze you with fear. Living fully in the present moment is the liberation of the Fool.

Words of Wisdom from the Fool Embrace the journey, trust the process, and uncover the wisdom of the Fool within.

Spirit Guide—Grasshopper The Grasshopper hops into your life, urging you to take that proverbial leap of faith, trusting the universe's embrace. Unfazed by the past, the Grasshopper can only hop forward, reminding you that what is behind you no longer matters; it's where you are going that counts.

Further Indulgence Grasshoppers dwell in the grass, with feet firmly planted, and are synonymous with grounding. Emulate the Grasshopper's essence: go barefoot, let your toes sink into the plushness of Mother Earth, and consciously connect with her grounding energies. Channel the spirit of the Grasshopper to nurture your own grounding practice.

I am so fresh in soul and spirit that life gushes and bubbles around me in a thousand springs.
Robert Schumann

1 The Magician

*Honing my dexterity,
with elemental magick I play
Conscious will channeled,
intentionally done my way
Skilled in misdirection, I'm the
master of slight of hand
A smile that enchants the masses,
do anything I command*

KEYWORDS & CONCEPTS

LIGHT: conscious, will, master, manifestation, confidence, dexterity, magick, intentional, talented, resolve, charismatic, competent, self-expressive, persuasive, cognizant, elemental magick, clever, empowered, adept

SHADOW: trickster, inept, magic, deceit, con man, shrewd, inconsiderate, illusion, misdirection, crafty, narcissistic, manipulation, intense, poser, awkward, elusive, chimera, arrogant, mistrust, occult, subterfuge, chameleon, sorcery, ambiguous

Scene On a quiet, desolate night, the Fox—enchanted with the essence of the Magician—emerges from his den precisely at midnight. He meticulously arranges his tools, eagerly anticipating your arrival. The Fox's ears perk up as he turns toward the sound of a twig snapping near the perimeter of the sacred circle. With an intense gaze, the Fox peers into the darkness, searching for signs of life, with unwavering determination. Cautiously approaching the Fox's lair, you try to regulate your breaths in an effort not to give away your presence. The Magician locks eyes with you, his stare sharp and perceptive. He acknowledges your presence with a smirk, his voice resonating with mischief and craft. "Ah, you've come," his words laced with an air of amusement. "Ready for your lesson, are you?" Your confidence wavers, as you feel a bead of sweat roll down your brow and into your eye, involuntarily winking at the Magician. He winks back. Horrified, your knees tremble, as you muster a strong reply: "Yes, I'm here, aren't I?" The Magician's eyes twinkle, and he chuckles softly, "Very well, my little grasshopper; let's begin."

The Magician shifts around and an air of intrigue rustles in the wind, bringing a curious smell to your nose. Channeling his magick, he raises his wand as a symphony of colorful energy emits from the tip, dancing like a curvy mistress and captivating your senses. Mesmerized, you watch as golden orbs shimmy harmoniously in the air. The Magician clears his throat to regain your attention, and in an arrogant voice he commands: "As above, so below. As within, so without. Always remember, you are the center of what it's all about." With a flourish of his hand, he presents the classical tools of fire, water, air, and earth. "These can be all yours to wield, for the special price of $369.00, guaranteed to master the elements or your money back!" Caught off guard by the offer, you stand there with your mouth gaping. Reality comes crashing in, and you shake your head, realizing the illusion has captivated you. Feeling foolish that you almost got conned, you mutter under your breath, "Fool!," not sure whether you meant it for him or you. As you turn to leave, maniacal laughter echoes through the twilight sky, sending shivers down your spine. Frozen for a moment in both fear and awe, you steal a glance over your shoulder before breaking out into a sprint, running the rest of the way home, questioning the boundaries of magick and reality.

Magician in Love A playboy at heart, the Magician finds adulting very unappealing; he'd rather stay single and young forever. Giving off major player vibes, when this master manipulator shows up . . . *RUN!*

Magician in Career A formidable presence, armed with a sharp mind and a skilled tongue, this coworker possesses an array of talents. But be cautious of their manipulative tendencies. They may come across as a know-it-all, adept at pulling your strings to further their own agenda.

Magician in Wellness Harness your innate power and embrace the enchanting realm of natural wellness. No fancy gadgets needed, your magickal essence is the key. Unleash your transformative abilities, crafting the best version of yourself inside and out. Radiate your authentic brilliance, leaving an indelible mark of magick on the world.

Magician in Finances Harness the power of manifestation and conscious wealth creation. Speak and think of money in a positive light, welcoming riches into your life. Accept assistance and take intentional action toward financial growth. Welcome a prosperous mindset, paving the way for the rivers of abundance to flow effortlessly.

The Magick of the Magician The Magician is the master of elemental magick, harnessing the power of air, fire, water, and earth in perfect harmony. Through spells that incorporate each element, call upon their assistance to manifest your desires. Remember to show gratitude to the wee beings with offerings of milk and honey for their support in your magickal endeavors.

Words of Wisdom from the Magician Don't die with your talents buried. You have been given all the tools necessary to create the amazing life you've always imagined.

Spirit Guide—Fox The cunning Fox comes loping onto your path, offering clarity and guidance. When you find yourself lost or entangled in illusions, call upon the Fox to reveal the way forward. Surrender to its wisdom and trust that it will lead you back to your true self, illuminating your next steps with purpose.

Further Indulgence Unleash the untamed power within as you delve into the realm of infinite possibilities. Embrace the ecstasy of exploration, be it through mystic rituals, intriguing quests, or daring self-expression. Immerse yourself in the forbidden arts, weave spells of enchantment, and dance with cosmic forces. Surrender to the allure of the unknown and become the alchemist of your own extraordinary existence.

Love is the magician that pulls man out his own hat.
Ben Hecht

2 The High Priestess

*Triple goddess of the realm,
guiding the lunar tide
Keeper of the ancient flame,
in snowy robes I glide
As an oracle of intuition,
seeds of foresight I sow
Gaze into my citrine eyes,
to uncover secrets I know*

KEYWORDS & CONCEPTS

LIGHT: intuition, secrets, premonition, mysterious, insight, the in-between, perception, ancient mysteries, spiritual connection, esoteric knowledge, inner wisdom, psychic medium, queen bee, dignified, oracle, all knowing, triple goddess, divine feminine

SHADOW: secrets, hindsight, foreboding, deception, suspicion, know-it-all, misconception, divulging secrets, premeditated, self-deception, ignoring intuition, grandiose, shortsighted, misconstrued, hidden motives, charlatan, seeing nothing, witchcraft

Scene Coming in the guise of the snowy white owl, the High Priestess appears before you as the keeper of the great work, priestess of the ancient mysteries, and the walker of the in-between. Crowned queen of the night, this guardian of the subconscious mind is always willing to teach worthy souls seeking initiation. Only those who stand before her in reverence will have access to the inner workings and secrets of the craft. Sitting between worlds on a velveteen moss throne amid the green lush woods, she drips with magick, treasures of great importance nestled close to her bosom. A tightly wrapped scroll harbors secret incantations; the pomegranate, the sacred symbol of Persephone, the embodiment of the divine feminine and the bearer of fruit. These are the same ruby-red sweet seeds that sustained Persephone, who once a year would leave the living and tread lightly upon the frosty earth, crossing the veil into the underworld, where once again she would reunite with her lover Hades as the rest of the world above slumbers in winter's grip. Seen beyond the misty veil, two pillars: one representing the divine feminine and the other the divine masculine. These energies stand sentinel, where only the ones that know how to apply Persephone's secrets will be granted access into the inner sanctum. The High Priestess's citrine eyes burn brightly, allowing her to see all things, both seen and unseen. As the daughter of the moon, an oracle to the masses, she peers through the inky darkness and into the recesses of your soul, silently observing what is hidden within its shadowy depths. Leaning in closer, she whispers softly, "Know thyself."

High Priestess in Love In the realm of love, hidden mysteries await those who are ready to embrace them. Like Persephone, the High Priestess patiently waits for the perfect time to reunite with her true love. Trust your intuition and be open to new love connections that may arrive with the fall of the first snow.

High Priestess in Career She excels in professions involving coaching, counseling, and providing guidance. With her captivating presence and deep wisdom, she brings a unique perspective to any workplace, offering valuable insights and making her a fascinating colleague to collaborate with.

High Priestess in Wellness Ruled by the Moon, the High Priestess guides you to honor the sacred rhythms of your body, including the life-giving blood of a woman's menstrual cycle. Embrace her wisdom and listen to your body; within those whispers lies the path to wellness. Your inner and outer journey awaits, illuminated by her lunar grace.

High Priestess in Finances Trust your instincts and make wise financial decisions with the guidance of the High Priestess. Seek opportunities for growth and stability, while staying attuned to the subtle rhythms of the market. Align your financial goals with your higher purpose and watch prosperity flow.

The Magick of the High Priestess Delve into the depths of your being, harnessing your innate psychic gifts to unveil the hidden truths yet to be discovered. Question everything, for not all is as it appears. Time has come to peer behind the veil, for there's strange energy afoot. Embrace the gifts of clairaudience and clairvoyance, attuning your ears to the unspoken words and hidden realities.

Words of Wisdom from the High Priestess "Know thyself." Delve into the depths of self-knowledge, commune with the mysterious oracle residing within, and cultivate the eternal flame of wisdom. For in knowing oneself, one finds the essence of existence and the gateway to profound enlightenment.

Spirit Guide—Snowy Owl The Snowy Owl is a majestic embodiment of magick and witchcraft and serves as a guardian of the ancient mysteries. The gift of second sight and the ability to turn its neck 270 degrees allows it to see every situation from all angles, unveiling hidden truths in plain sight. Invite its presence as it guides you to unravel deeper layers of energy and unlock the intuition that lies within.

Further Indulgence Dive deep into indulgence, surrendering to the seductive allure of the High Priestess. Unleash your desires and let the divine feminine bloom like pomegranate seeds, as you explore your sensual depths within. Embrace the intoxicating magick, embody your sexual essence, and revel in the forbidden pleasures that ignite your soul's passion.

> *She is our moon—our tidal pull. She is the rich deep*
> *beneath the sea, the buried treasure, the expression in the*
> *owl's eye, the perfume in the wild rose.*
> *She is what the water says when it moves.*
> **Patricia A. McKillip**

3 The Empress

Nurturing the spark of life within,
my belly brims with grace
In the flow of rightful existence,
serenity finds her place
With gentle touch, vibrant blooms
grow, nature's colorful plume
Creating space for fertility,
embracing life's abundant room

KEYWORDS & CONCEPTS

LIGHT: fertility, full of love, feminine, ample, possibility, maternal, beauty, yielding, fruitful, graceful, nurturing, selfless, abundance, the mother, soft, creatrix, matriarch, pregnancy, growing, green mother

SHADOW: barren, mushy, cold, overbearing, lacking, selfish lover, smother, empty, something's missing, overprotective, wanting, obligatory love, infertility, mommy issues, neglect, shallow, manipulative

Scene On a lush grassy knoll the Empress is seated on a cool earthen floor among the daisies, on an especially warm spring day. Her woolly head supports a grand headdress befitting her station as Mother of the Realm. Crowns filled with fragrant flowers are wrapped in lovely pearls, regally nestled between her deadly horns. Casually, she glances toward her offspring and her soul fills with love, resting easy, knowing that this magickal maternal bond cannot be severed. Today's a special day, for the Highland Cow gave birth to a beautiful baby calf, ensuring the survival of many future generations yet to come. Ceremoniously the Empress affixes a delicate daisy chain to adorn the brow of her proudest accomplishment; looking into the soulful

eyes of her charge, she says: "I am so grateful for the privilege of bringing you through me. As you move through life, there will be both happiness and hardships. Be reverent to both equally, for they'll be experiences chosen by your soul. Always remember, this is your life that's lived for you, and you alone. Never bow a knee or play small, for you are a star. I promise to always be there, to guide you, and to love you enough to let you go, since I would never intervene with your soul's journey." And with that, the Highland Cow dropped a gentle kiss atop her baby's soft head. Blinking, the new soul looks up at the grandness of the woman before her and slowly blinks her brown eyes in agreement. The baby calf nestles even closer, pressing her body into the softness of the Empress's fuzzy fur, fully closing her heavy lids and falling asleep feeling warm, safe, and loved.

Empress in Love The embodiment of unconditional motherly love invites you to embrace the raw beauty of connection. Remind yourself that when you find "your person," embrace the profound beauty of their soul, allowing experiences to unfold naturally, unencumbered by human constraints.

Empress in Career The Empress gracefully carries her abundant talents and nurturing gifts into the workplace, quickly becoming everyone's mom. Her creativity knows no bounds, and her ability to adapt and learn fuels her achievements, as she effortlessly manifests success. With a plethora of ideas and an open attitude, she thrives in any endeavor she sets her mind on.

Empress in Wellness Embrace the healing power of nature, immersing yourself in the splendor of Earth's bounty. Connect your soles to her body, touching the trees, singing with the birds, and healing yourself in her waters. Let the earth breathe life into your being, revitalizing your spirit and nurturing your wellness.

Empress in Finances The Empress ignites abundance in your financial endeavors, opening the door to a comfortable and abundant flow of money. Embrace her energy to ignite projects with great potential that bloom into long-term financial success, offering opportunities for passive income and fulfilling financial future. Trust in the fertile ground you stand upon, and nurture your financial growth.

The Magick of the Empress The magick of the Empress lies in her ability to manifest abundance effortlessly. She harnesses the power of creation, nurturing dreams into reality. Embrace her energy, trust your instincts, and witness the enchantment unfold as your desires blossom with grace and beauty.

Words of Wisdom from the Empress When you do everything with love, you will reap from the fullness of life in the form of abundance.

Spirit Guide—Highland Cow Imposing yet elegant, this hairy Cow emerges adorned with daisy crowns and carrying seeds of eternal life. With every step, she sows seeds of wildflowers entangled in her hairs, leaving a trail of blossoming blessings. Embrace their presence, dance in the sun, and let daisies be strewn under your feet, for you, too, deserve the beauty of nature's embrace.

Further Indulgence Place you hands on your belly, connecting with the ember within. Breathe life into the spark, igniting a raging inferno of desire. The Empress embodies artistic creation, channeling imagination into reality. Harness this technique to inspire the manifestation of your deepest creative aspirations.

I cast a glance in my new admirer's direction.
"You may call me Your Highness," I said. "Or Empress Beauty."
He chuckled. I wasn't kidding.
Gena Showalter

4 The Emperor

*Unyielding in my reign,
resolute and bold
A sovereign of authority,
as legends unfold
Unfazed by other's thoughts,
firm in decree
The crown on my head declares,
Emperor I be*

KEYWORDS & CONCEPTS

LIGHT: ruler, paternal, hardened, dutiful, regimented, father figure, secure, masculine, stoic, experienced, mature, patriarch, leader, protector, king of kings, fearless, alpha, powerful, tenacious, action oriented, strategic thinker

SHADOW: unyielding, dictator, tyrant, militant, controlling, domination, battle-scarred, insatiable, barbaric, inflexible, ruthless, authoritarian, pompous, emasculating, attitude, commander, arrogance, strict, daddy issues

Scene Among the thickets and overgrown vines, the Emperor sits in his seat of power, overtaken by life. The aliveness of the greenery makes him acutely familiar of the parts inside that have died long ago. He's painfully aware of the weighty stone left behind, where his heart once used to beat. Cramming his oversized body into a stone throne and curling his iron fist tightly over the ornate handles, he feels the coolness under the pads of his calloused fingers. Scenes of the past flash before his eyes; too much time has lapsed since his last battle, leaving him struggling to regain his rightful place. Overcome with frustration, he jumps up, baring his teeth while profusely pounding on his chest, growling so loudly that the barbaric sound bounces

off the trees, reverberating throughout the woods. He shouts into the emptiness of night, "How can I be the man I am supposed to be, without acknowledging the man I once was?" The problem is, he's viewed as the hardened mature Emperor; forgotten is the Gorilla warrior who's lying just beneath the surface. As time marched on, old wounds flared up, and he became so disheartened that he stopped trying to heal altogether. He thinks back to the days of battle when he would've done anything just to be shown a shred of kindness. But today, even with all the adoration, it makes his stomach turn and hurdle. What he would give to be able to bleed so he can feel something, anything. The tension held in his jawline suddenly gave way to his own resolve. Finally facing the truth, he's now able to let go of his painful past, burying the stone heart and letting it return back to the earth. A new feeling began to spread across his chest, as he feels a first beat, and then another, until a symphony of rhythmic thuds followed in sequence. Picking up his crown and placing it on his head, he looks into the distance and reclaims his throne as Emperor of the realm, loving father to all creatures, and dutiful protector of future generations. Accepting this fate, his Gorilla warrior settles down, as man and beast merge to become one great Emperor. He turns his face toward the future with a hopeful heart.

Emperor in Love Once you have penetrated the inner sanctum of the Emperor's heart, you're in for life. When the Emperor loves, he loves hard, but in the same breath he's very hard to love . . . and this is where the conundrum lies. Being a defensive type of card, it's challenging to get close to someone like the Emperor, but not impossible.

Emperor in Career As an emblem of authority and leadership, the Emperor thrives in a career where he can be the driving force, making the decisions and setting a clear path for others to follow. His strong work ethic makes him a natural fit for roles that require structure and organization. With the ability to command respect, the Emperor demands loyalty from his subordinates.

Emperor in Wellness The Emperor's strong and assertive nature extends to his approach to wellness. He values discipline and physical strength, emphasizing the importance of maintaining a strong, healthy body. By incorporating a structured fitness routine and taking proactive measures to address any bodily aches and stiffness, this Emperor will thrive.

Emperor in Finances Ruling over finances with a firm hand, the Emperor promotes stability and strategic planning. His disciplined approach, coupled with his ability to make practical decisions, leads to financial success and establishing a solid financial empire.

The Magick of the Emperor Experience has brought you this far; assess the situation with a calm demeanor before taking action. Keep a cool head, for it is in composure that true reason resides. Embrace the stability and grounding energy of hematite, the stone of the Emperor.

Words of Wisdom from the Emperor Rely on the culmination of your experiences, embrace the wisdom to adapt when needed, and witness the grandeur of your empire unfold.

Spirit Guide—Silverback Gorilla This gentle giant brings the gift of unwavering loyalty, for when provoked, the Silverback Gorilla transforms into a ferocious beast and will go to any lengths to fiercely defend those he loves. He will stand by your side, an indomitable presence, guiding and guarding you through life's trials with unyielding strength and determination.

Further Indulgence Embrace the thorns and roses of life with unwavering resolve, for within them lie the lessons of the Emperor. Pound on your chest and release your inner resounding roar; let go of what's hindering your growth. Face challenges with resolute determination and find the beauty and power in every experience. The Emperor meets you on your path, giving you the power to assert your dominion over destiny.

You put this steel armor around yourself in the
form of hostility and disinterest—whichever works to shield
you best at the moment, but that's not who you are.
Pauline Creeden

5 The Hierophant

*In sacred rites,
the mysteries unfold
Teacher and advisor,
wise and bold
Philosophical crow,
guiding with grace
Unveiling wisdom in
ceremonial embrace*

KEYWORDS & CONCEPTS

LIGHT: hierarchy, philosophy, wisdom, mentorship, religion, spirit guide, advisor, principled, ceremonial, compliance, traditional, rituals, institutions, conscientious, patient, conventional, morality, council, doctrine, knowledgeable

SHADOW: gatekeeper, shallow, unethical, fanatical, indoctrination, repression, immoral, skeptic, dogmatist, unconventional, superstitious, bad advice, no answers, initiate

Scene It's one fine afternoon, and class is in session as the Hierophant ceremoniously perches himself on the soft, mossy mound. Proudly wearing a golden helmet befitting his station as Gatekeeper of the Realms, he sees into both physical and spiritual worlds. Heavily draped around his inky neck are the Keys to the Kingdom, which unlock many realms and parallel universes. Silence befalls the initiates looking on with shining eyes full of admiration, eagerly hanging on to the teacher's every word. Clearing his throat, the teacher speaks: "Everything hangs in the balance on a slivered razor's edge, bridging the in-between. And yet, in the same instance, bouncing off perceived

distances of polar opposites, entangled in one giant exhale of a single moment in time." The initiates nervously look at each other, with no clue to what the teacher just said. The Crow, his eyes alit with knowledge, addresses the class once again: "Initiates, hands up if you believe that everything happens for a reason, and all things experienced are preordained. Do we all agree?" The Hierophant scans the group, ensuring all hands are raised. Smiling he continues, "Initiates! I possess all answers to any question, knowing all outcomes to every possibility, *correct*?" Purposefully nodding his head, four little heads nod back in unison. "Right! And how do we get these answers, class? Do we ask the teacher?" Four little voices recite, "No, Hierophant. You give guidance. We must find the answers for ourselves." Satisfied, the Hierophant slowly nods, tilting his head, as the helmet pulsated with knowledge. Unexpectedly, a deep silence befell the class. As tensions built, the Hierophant slowly raised an eyebrow, abruptly shouting, "WHY?" Startling the little group, they answered with gusto, "BECAUSE WE MUST LEARN FOR OURSELVES!" The Crow, straightening himself to full height and spreading his wings, smiles and says, "Class dismissed!"

Hierophant in Love In each lifetime, ordained encounters hold profound purpose. The Hierophant's presence signals a divine lesson in love. Pay heed to its guidance, for it orchestrates meaningful connections and unveils truths from other lifetimes. If single, this card indicates that you will find true love later in life.

Hierophant in Career Dive deeper into the realm of knowledge, for the Hierophant unveils the power of continuous learning. Embrace the mantle of a wise teacher by sharing your expertise, while emulating the eternal student with more job training.

Hierophant in Wellness Find joy in every task, even the ones that are duties, for they hold hidden lessons. The Hierophant guides you to find purpose in everything, and to thwart procrastination and unnecessary stress.

Hierophant in Finances The Hierophant signifies prudent investments, disciplined budgeting, and seeking reliable financial advice to fulfill your financial goals.

The Magick of the Hierophant In sacred rituals and traditions lies the magick of the Hierophant. Unlock spiritual wisdom by finding solace in ancient teachings and connect with higher realms. Manifest divine blessings through the power of traditions to create a magickal transformation.

Words of Wisdom from the Hierophant Embody the wisdom of tradition, but don't be bound by it. Seek knowledge, ask questions, and write your own story.

Spirit Guide—The Crow The Crow comes cawing into your life as a symbol of wisdom and mysticism, inviting you to see beyond the ordinary and embrace the extraordinary mysteries of life. Bringing the gift of transformative energy, the Crow guides you to explore deeper spiritual truths and unlock hidden knowledge held within. The Crow teaches us to trust our intuition and connect with higher realms of understanding.

Further Indulgence Immerse yourself in the sacred art of penning your thoughts upon the pages of a journal. Capture divine wisdom through reflection as the ink bleeds into the threads of the tapestry, guiding your spiritual growth with a gentle hand of profound teachings. Reflect, evolve, and embody the wisdom of the Hierophant's sacred path.

Two things are infinite:
the universe and human stupidity; and I'm not so
sure about the universe.
Albert Einstein

6 The Lovers

In the tapestry of destiny, our souls will forever be entwined
Neither time nor space can sever the bond, that true love defined
Lovers and lifetimes woven together will always find a way
Back in each other's arms, bound eternally in love we stay

KEYWORDS & CONCEPTS

LIGHT: lovers, together, eroticism, choices (love), worthy of love, love connection, respect, desire, soulmates, attraction, arrangement, divine love, sexual, romance, sensuality, falling in love, trust

SHADOW: lust, forbidden, binding spell, codependency, tainted love, lacking interest, unrequited love, no choice, disrespected, love out of duty, betrayal, contract, boredom, affair, vulnerable to love scams

Scene A pair of Lovebirds hold each other, tired from the day's festivities, for today was the most joyous of all occasions, their mating ceremony. Forever binding the soulmates together with love, unto death and beyond. It all began when she heard his soul calling, one fateful night when she found him alone, sleeping in the rain. She watched over him until the break of day, until the sunshine came and chased the darkness away. Satisfied he was safe in the light, she took one last glance and flew away. Years flew by, then one day she found him again. Something familiar danced on the edge of her consciousness, but in that moment she couldn't recall. The instant he saw her, a familiar

scent made his heart skip, as a premonition washed over him that something wonderful is happening. Bodies touching, and talking about the best of times and the worst, under the ever watchful eye of the moon, laughing when in the morning they greeted the sun. It was in that moment a memory came alive, seen from his eyes, of a fateful night so long ago. He told her of the worst night of his life, where he slept in the rain, disoriented and alone. Suddenly, everything fell into place for her—it was him that night! She shared how she watched him from afar sleeping in the rain, compelled to stay until the sun came and chased the darkness away. Immediately looking deeply into each other's souls, as realization dawned upon the Lovebirds, he whispered, "I was born to love you." She replied, "And I was made for you." From that day forward they were inseparable; wherever she went, he followed; where he was, she was right there with him. Bonded forever, every day was a gift filled with love and happiness as they spent their days kissing in the sun, their nights singing to the moon, and, every chance they'd get, dancing in the rain.

Lovers in Love If in a relationship, passionately embrace and celebrate each other's presence. Nurture the flame of love and recognize its undying power. Know that no force can sever the bond between soulmates who are destined for eternal connection. If single, trust in divine timing. You will be united with your mate.

Lovers in Career The Lovers card in career represents finding a true calling and deep passion for your work. It can also indicate the presence of romantic or sexual connection in the workplace, whether with a coworker or a superior.

Lovers in Wellness Heal and nourish your heart on all levels: physical, emotional, and spiritual. Recognize the significance of the heart as the center of your being and the embodiment of love. When your heart is beating, you are alive; when it stops, so do you. Keep going.

Lovers in Finances The Lovers card in finances reveals the power of strategic choices. Embrace opportunities that align with your financial goals and values. Forge partnerships and investments rooted in passion and purpose. Nurture a harmonious relationship with money for lasting abundance and profound fulfillment.

The Magick of the Lovers Within the infinite spiral dance of soulmates, two beautiful souls descend to Earth, embodying the essence of love. When blessed with the fleeting experience of such a profound connection, it etches itself into your being, designed for reunion in eternity. Love's magick transcends time, binding souls eternally.

Words of Wisdom from the Lovers You never should have to beg someone to stay. If they love you, they won't leave you.

Spirit Guide—Lovebird Lovebirds, the enchanting messengers of love, bring the gift of harmony and companionship. Their tender bond reflects the essence of soulmates and the power of unconditional love. They soar through life together, inspiring you to cherish the connections that ignite your heart and nurture the flame of love from within.

Further Indulgence Immerse yourself in the graceful flow of dance, mirroring the Lovebirds' symbiotic movements. Let their rhythm inspire you to embrace the art of dance, allowing its fluidity to awaken your spirit.

True love stories never have endings.
Richard Bach

7 The Chariot

*Guided by ambition's fire,
I steer the road ahead
Focused on the path before me,
not easily misled
With purpose and control,
I hold fate's reigns tight
Driven by sheer determination,
and unwavering might*

KEYWORDS & CONCEPTS

LIGHT: activation, self-governance, determination, control, vehicle, handler, driving force, self-restraint, sense of direction, road map, time travel, focus, progress, ambition, motivation, going places, the road ahead, opposites attract

SHADOW: someone else is holding the reigns, uncommitted, mind control, lost, out of control, puppeteer, unruly, agenda, time machine, useless, unmanageable, one-track mind, runaway train, inconsistent effort

Scene The Chariot is packed and ready to go, as the Zebra begins his journey into the depths of the dark woods. The lantern's dim glow shines just enough light for him to see only one step at a time; as for the one after that, he has to rely on himself, trusting the next step will appear. Focused on treading softly, so as not to trample the daisies underfoot, the Zebra makes steady progress, relying on his great sense of direction to safely guide him through. As he walks forth in silence, he finds himself deep in thought, taking an inventory of his life. He feels excitement course through his body for what might be waiting for him just beyond the grove. He's heard interesting things about the new world, a place where until recently he never knew existed. Suddenly the topography changes. Ahead the road is densely lined with tall structures made of stone. Abruptly stopping before a red-and-white barrier blocking his path, the Zebra looks around perplexed, since he must have crossed over into a different time: everything looks so different, gray and cold. Gone is the aliveness and vibrancy of the woods. "Where you heading?" The order is barked by a militant-looking human, his face reading just how unimpressed he is. The Zebra straightens up to full height and looks the creature dead in the eyes and says, "I've come from afar, bringing the Chariot forth; I am to be the transportation for the one you all refer to as the Greatest of All Time. Grant me safe passage, so I can fulfill my destiny." The guard suspiciously eyes the Chariot, walking slowly around, lifting flaps, looking inside the saddlebags strapped onto the Zebra's sides. Satisfied, the guard returns to his post, picks up the radio, and says, "Sir, your Chariot awaits," while waving the Zebra through. The Chariot slowly and intentionally rolls through the threshold, crossing the portal, ready to make history.

Chariot in Love When a significant decision has to be made, have the courage to see it through. Once the wheels have been set in motion, there's no turning back. For those seeking love, keep making steady progress toward your relationship goals and create opportunities for love to enter your life.

Chariot in Career When you're asking about a career, the Chariot signifies a time of forward momentum and assertive action. Take the reins of your professional journey and steer it with confidence and restraint. See challenges as opportunities for growth and let your ambition propel you toward success. Trust your instincts, stay focused, and strive for excellence as you navigate the road map to achieving your career goals. As far as a specific career, the Chariot represents the transportation industry and all modes of movement.

Chariot in Wellness Things are progressing. Look to the surrounding cards to see in what direction everything is heading when inquiring about health and wellness.

Chariot in Finances Forge ahead with determination toward financial success. Navigate decisions wisely, gathering information and aligning actions with your goals. Drive your finances in the direction of victory.

The Magick of the Chariot Garner the magick of the Chariot by embarking on a meditative journey. Take a moment to visualize yourself conquering a personal challenge, overcoming obstacles with resolve and courage. Find your inner strength and take action moving toward your desire.

Words of Wisdom from the Chariot So, I guess this is goodbye. Thank you for all the lessons you've taught me. I promise to wear my battle scars with pride. Maybe one day our paths my cross, but don't be surprised when I pay you no mind, because I've moved on with my life.

Spirit Guide—Zebra The Zebra comes embodying the gift of balance, enforced by the qualities of individuality and adaptability. It reminds you to embrace your uniqueness, navigate life's challenges with grace, and find harmony in contrasting ideals. The Zebra guides you toward embracing your diversity and walking your own authentic path.

Further Indulgence Immerse yourself in the beauty of duality. Embrace the contrasting stripes within you, for they create a unique tapestry of intertwining threads. Be adaptable, bold, and unafraid to stand out in the crowd. Find balance in between the movement of the light and shadow.

If everything seems under control, you're just not going fast enough.
Mario Andretti

8 Strength

*Snarling, showing my incisors,
I wield my inner might
Fearlessly confronting challenges,
pursuing what is right
Unyielding in my beliefs,
confidence shining through
Discover your own strength within,
for it resides in you*

KEYWORDS & CONCEPTS

LIGHT: strength, endurance, survivalist, brave, confidence, courageous, fortitude, intensity, creativity, formidable, resilience, power, toughness, lionhearted, tenacity, willpower unwavering, gentleness, assertive

SHADOW: weakness, overcritical, egotistical, inner turmoil, apathetic, pride, aggressive, feigned strength, extremist, brutal, attention seeker, nonchalant, insistent, forceful, issues with authority figures, dominance

Scene On a beautiful summer's day, the Dire Wolf feels the warm breeze rush over her fur, rustling the silky hairs and awaking her body to the most wonderful sensation. She's the best they have; they call her Strength, and she wears the moniker with pride. As Protector of the Realm, she wears a magickal helmet adorned with the most beautiful intricate design, steeped in magickal spells. Suddenly a scent snaps her out of her daydream. Tilting her nose in the air to pick up the scent, it is one she knows oh too well: the deer is coming. "Three, two, one, and . . ." Right on cue, "Hi, Strength! I was just passing by and thought I'd pop in." Strength looked over at her friend, rolling her eyes.

"What do you want, Buck?" The deer became slightly crestfallen, since he even wore his extra-special cape for her today. "Strength, can you please tell me the story, please?" Strength's heart immediately softened when she looked at her friend's curious choice of attire. "Okay, Buck. I'll tell you the story again. And by the way, you like nice today." The deer kicked up his front legs giving Strength a high five and saying, "Nailed it!" Strength raised a paw and chuckled, then began to tell the story. "Since a small cub, I've always known I was destined for greatness. When I was old enough to join the competition, I did, beating out the most seasoned of warriors for the title 'Protector of the Realm.'" The Buck interrupts, "But why did they choose you?" The Dire Wolf gave the Buck a sidelong look, watching him turn a deep shade of red that matched his cape. Immediately the Buck looked away, fiddling with his cape, and quietly said, "You know, being a girl and all—who's never even seen a battle—why you?" The Dire Wolf levels her bright-yellow eyes and looks the Buck right in the mouth: "Strength comes in all forms. I demonstrated I can be ferocious but fair, courageous yet careful, and tough, but still knowing when a gentle touch is needed. I know how to survive and take care of myself. I also stand up for the ones who cannot stand for themselves." The Buck's eyes shone with admiration for his friend, satisfied with the answer. He quickly said goodbye and dashed on his way. "See you soon, Buck." As Strength's goodbye fell into the wind, she mumbled under her breath, "When you'll be back tomorrow, asking the same question again." Smiling to herself, Strength went right back to basking in the sun. She closed her eyes and drifted off to sleep.

Strength in Love Strength brings an intense energy into any relationship, amplifying the current dynamic, which can be both pleasurable and distasteful. One advantage is that you'll always know what Strength is thinking and feeling, for they're confident partners who have no problem telling you exactly how they feel. If single, focus on building self-confidence to attract strong and authentic connections.

Strength in Career A born leader who naturally gravitates toward prestigious titles or careers, they are the boss and in complete control, with the final say. The way to get through that tough standoffish exterior is with compliments, undying loyalty, and admiration for their greatness, and in a flash you'll be their new pet.

Strength in Wellness Focus on building Strength by regularly engaging in weight training that targets both small and large muscle groups.

Strength in Finances The power of financial freedom takes center stage for this card, exuding confidence in the realm of finances. They possess an insatiable need to maintain a firm grip over all financial affairs and transactions.

The Magick of Strength You are pure energy, a timeless soul. Tune into your sacred inner sanctuary of love and peace. Embody confidence in the knowledge that all will be well. Believe in Strength and accept that whatever is happening right now is exactly what you need for growth.

Words of Wisdom from Strength With unwavering determination and immense power, I will conquer any challenge that comes my way. Watch me rise to greatness!

Spirit Guide—Dire Wolf The spirit of the Dire Wolf brings the gift of primal instincts accompanied by loyalty and fierce protection. It serves as a reminder to trust your strengths, stay true to your pack, and fearlessly defend what is important to you. Let your wild nature be your guide.

Further Indulgence Embody the qualities of Strength by embracing the power within. Begin with a strong desire and unwavering determination, sprinkled with hard work. Take time to reflect on your deepest desires through meditation, asking yourself what you truly want in this lifetime. This clarity will guide you toward achieving the impossible.

The lion may be more powerful,
but the wolf does not perform in the circus.
Anonymous

9 The Seeker

*Guided by my lantern's glow,
I walk paths yet unknown
A journey of pensive solitude,
where true wisdom is sown
Through introspection and discovery,
I travel wide and far
Patiently seeking enlightenment,
following my guiding star*

KEYWORDS & CONCEPTS

LIGHT: wisdom, solitary, introspection, remote, inner guidance, silence, maturity, pensiveness, stillness, contemplation, patience, enlightenment, reflection, observation, lantern of illumination

SHADOW: shallowness, thoughtlessness, isolation, narrow-minded, withdrawn, misinformed, shortsighted, withdrawal, dismissive, apathetic, cacophony, loneliness, absentminded, aimless wanderer

Scene Following the quiet roll of the river, roaming around with no particular destination, the Grizzly Bear is on a solo path of enlightenment. Pensive in solitude, with only his thoughts to keep him company, he searches for the pieces of himself he lost long ago. Peacefully strolling along, he's enjoying the quietness of the evening and the freedoms that detachment affords.

Comfortable in his skin, he embarks on this reflective journey, for the Seeker's intentions of aloneness are purposeful. He's not sad or lonely, for his past experience allows him the ease of patience, as he continues to follow his inner compass. Under a twilight sky, his sapphire robe catches the glow

of the lantern's diffused light in just the right way, casting a golden halo around the Grizzly's head, highlighting his capacity for introspection. Unattached and alone, he continues down his soul's path, seeking knowledge and connection within. Once attained, he can then shine an even brighter light from his lantern of illumination, out into the world. The calm demeanor of the Seeker is revealed by his gentle energy, lumbering along, never quick to jump to any conclusions or to pass judgment. Although the Grizzly can be quite ferocious when provoked, he favors a more peaceful nature. This gentle giant prefers to keep his council, making it the quintessential card for never mistaking someone's silence for weakness, since silence is deadly in the presence of an enlightened mind. The Seeker pauses, looking straight ahead, and whispers into the darkness, "Sapere aude."

Seeker in Love Preferring his own company, the Seeker is content to be alone, for the truth is, it's very possible to feel lonely within a relationship. He doesn't want to settle, knowing that in order to attract lasting love, you must first learn love yourself.

Seeker in Career The Seeker thrives in solitary pursuits, finding success in career paths that involve working alone and leveraging specialized knowledge through dedicated research. When collaborating with others, he prioritizes personal space in order to maintain productivity and contribute effectively to the team. The Seeker avoids loud environments, recognizing the importance of silence when quest setting for his work to thrive.

Seeker in Wellness Take your time and embrace the wisdom of knowing when to be gentle with yourself, or when you need to push through challenges. Reflect of your own journey, listen to your inner voice, and navigate toward your true north.

Seeker in Finances Dive deep into research and analysis, seeking hidden opportunities and innovative strategies. Take calculated risks, sizing advantageous moments while staying grounded. Trust yourself; you will learn both from your wins and loses.

The Magick of the Seeker The time has come for you to embrace solitude and delve deeper into introspection. It's through this inner journey that clarity awaits, allowing yourself to commune with guides and rediscover your purpose. The Seeker's magickal prowess lies in remote viewing, so turn your outward perception inward and find out where the true magick resides.

Words of Wisdom from the Seeker It is impossible to destroy someone who uses their greatest tragedies in life to fuel their next greatest quest.

Spirit Guide—Grizzly Bear The Grizzly Bear challenges you to tap into the energy of the star formation above the lantern, Ursa Major. It guides you to explore your subconscious and conscious mind. During this period of hibernation, avoid getting too comfortable sleeping your time away. Welcome the stillness, to plant seeds of tomorrow, while preparing for powerful manifestations upon awakening.

Further Indulgence In the depth of solitude, the lantern's glow reveals answers to your questions. Immerse yourself in introspective activities such as journaling, reading, or connecting with nature. Adopt the Seeker's craft to unlock the wisdom within, to assist on your solitary journey.

Solitude is unbearable for those who cannot bear themselves.
John Lancaster Spalding

10 The Wheel of Fortune

*On Destiny's spin,
Fortune's wheel reveals her face
Round and round she dances,
weaving at a mystic pace
The hand that rocks the cradle twists
the threads of fate
Some soul experiences are woven,
and some you cocreate*

KEYWORDS & CONCEPTS

LIGHT: chance, fate, cycles of life, reincarnation, kismet, passage of time, turning point, fortune, recurring, destiny, serendipity, repeating, Lady Luck, alignment, gamble, horoscope, providence, change, opportunity

SHADOW: no dice, going along for the ride, doldrums of life, fluke, hardship, bad karma, dire straits, unlikely, bad luck, stuck in a rut, unlucky, repeating, unmotivated, spinning, twist of fate, life's ups and downs

Scene On a hot, sultry summer's eve, at the edge of a riverbank the Wheel spins on its axis, marking the seasonal quarters. Beginning at the top is the spring equinox, when everything's fresh and new, symbolized by the fuzzy yellow duckling. Returning to life after a long winter's slumber, the duckling tries peeping to get the bee's attention. "Hey, Bee! Hope you're ready for summer solstice, because the Wheel is turning next toward you!" Buzzing back, the Bee acknowledges the new soul and says, "I'm ready. I've been working hard preparing and pollinating the flowers to insure the continuance of life."

The busy Bee winks at the duckling and continues working diligently, because before you know it, the great Wheel of Fortune will turn once again. The Bee looks to the Squirrel buried under a pile of leaves and says, "Get up, lazy bones; the Wheel's turning again! You must collect the bounty before fall equinox. You know the rule: what you don't gather before then must remain and be given back to the earth. Squirrel, come on, get up!" The Squirrel, all cozy and warm, tried burrowing even deeper into the rut. But she was rudely awakened by a buzzing in her ear. She slightly cracked open an eye, and yawned, looking skeptically at the Bee. "Yeah, yeah, I'm ready, Bee. Just taking a wee nap, you know, slowing down with the season. Don't concern yourself with me, for I've been through all this before."

The Squirrel quickly turns to face the Arctic Fox. "Hey, old chap, I see you've donned your winter solstice coat. The weather's really starting to turn. The Wheel's spinning your way. Are you ready, friend?" The Arctic Fox glances toward the center of the clock, where the hands are pointing to 10:10 p.m. The sun set awhile ago, and it's less than two hours before New Year's. When the time comes, he looks up, addressing the Duckling. "I'm ready. The time is neigh for me to leave, and at the same instance, I will have arrived."

And with that, the Wheel completed one whole revolution, ending the year and beginning anew.

The Wheel of Fortune in Love Symbolizes a pivotal moment in relationships, acknowledging the serendipitous nature of love. When the Wheel of Fortune shows up, cycles of fate and destiny are at play. Stay open to new connections and opportunities. Trust the wheel's constant motion, bringing unexpected joys and change when it comes to love.

The Wheel of Fortune in Career The Wheel spins, bringing major changes happening in the workplace. Hold on, this will be a bumpy and wild ride! Through this, a new opportunity or lucky break will soon present itself as the Wheel turns over, beginning another cycle.

The Wheel of Fortune in Wellness The Wheel of Fortune brings shifts and fluctuation in your health-and-wellness journey. The key is to accept change and trust the process. Stay open to new approaches and opportunities to improve your well-being. Movement and flexibility will be paramount to maintaining stamina during this transformational time.

The Wheel of Fortune in Finances The Wheel brings financial gambles, where luck is on your side. You may experience winning some money, a lucky opportunity, or an unexpected inheritance resulting in favorable outcomes. Embrace fortune's twists and turns as your financial situation improves.

The Magick of the Wheel of Fortune Harness the energy of the spinning Wheel by lighting a candle and reciting this mantra: "I embrace the flow of destiny, surrendering to its twists and turns. With every revolution, I realign with my true purpose, by embracing transformation as I follow my soul's path."

Words of Wisdom from the Wheel The only constant in life is change! Embrace change, for within the ever-turning hands of fate lies the power to transform your life. Trust in the cycles of destiny and seize the opportunities that come your way.

Spirit of the Wheel of Fortune The Wheel of Fortune spins under the watchful gaze of Lady Luck, weaving her web of unpredictable fate. It heralds serendipitous moments, teaching you to embrace both auspicious and challenging outcomes, for within the reel of the goddess Tyche's sacred dance lies the wisdom of life's grand tapestry.

Further Indulgence Indulge in the enchantment of the ever-turning Wheel, where nature's symphony weaves the seasons of life. Create a seasonal altar adorned with corresponding symbols, to honor the passage of time. Immerse yourself in the delights of seasonal food, engage in joyous celebration, and be captivated by the changes that each season brings.

To fate and the strange way that it twists us all together.
Nora Roberts

11 Justice

Before me you stand,
Justice rains upon your head
Karma's hand delivers,
by all things done and said
Some words stay around longer
than physical acts
My decision is based in ordinance,
strictly on facts

KEYWORDS & CONCEPTS

LIGHT: justice, good karma, legal matters, truth, karmic laws, fairness, decisions, balancing the scales, symmetry, weighing pros and cons, equilibrium, facts, responsibility, contracts and documents, integrity, awareness, know your rights

SHADOW: judgment, bad karma, prejudice, unfairness, illegal, bias, corruption, lawlessness, unjust, imbalance, intolerance, unfair outcome, unaware, problems with contracts and documents, consequence, ordinance, abuse of power

Scene Justice stood in the center of the world, wearing the Hat of Scales, humming to the cosmos below:

Cause and effect, the swinging of the scales.
Karma is a coldhearted bitch, who never fails.

With that said, then the white Crane lowers her head, taking measure of a soul suddenly appearing before her, a shell of a man begging her to let him go back for a chance to make things right with his son, wanting to see him grow. Amused, the Crane looks at him and says, "This is a game you're not going to win, but you keep rolling the dice in hopes of a better lot." Slowly shaking her head, she shrugs her shoulders and softly chuckles, "Human nature, I guess." The soul steadily looks at Justice, for fear of breaking eye contact and being perceived as weak. The hands of time tick on, seeming like infinity, when in truth it's an infinitesimal moment at best. An idea crests into the Crane's awareness as she poses a question to the man: "Well, then I ask you, human, what's in a teeny, tiny moment anyway?" She raises a perfectly arched eyebrow in inquiry. The man, now visibly uncomfortable, feels it's a trap, not knowing how to answer correctly. He gives up, lowers his head, and says nothing at all. Justice spreads her wings, ruffling her feathers to shake off excess tension. Respecting his silence, she states, "Ah, good. Now, let me tell you what's in a moment . . . *EVERYTHING!*" The man's confused expression says it all as the Crane continues. "As Justice, I mete out the effect to your cause. I never judge, but I act, so *EVERYTHING* hangs in the balanced breath of a moment." The man's eyes brighten with understanding, and he says in a clear voice, "I wish to go back! This moment! Right now!" And with that, the Crane smiles and says, "Now, Justice is served." She starts calibrating and shifting the scales, sending the man where he deserves to be. In an instance, the man was standing before Justice, and now he's caught up in a spinning psychedelic blur, until, with everything abruptly stopped, the man cautiously opens his eyes and gasps!

Justice in Love In the realm of love, Justice weaves the karmic threads entwining two souls in a lovers' embrace. Karma unveils harmonious connections or reveals lessons untold. Welcome recurring challenges, for they persist until love's true path is chosen, igniting profound soul love within your being.

Justice in Career In the realm of career, Justice guides your path with a demand for balance. Share the workload, strive for work-life balance, and seek a career aligned with the principles of law and justice for ultimate fulfillment.

Justice in Wellness Justice is ruled by the Law of Karma, where her actions echo through your body. Your wise blood holds the truth, unveiling the consequences of your choices. Embrace this truth to restore balance and harmony to your being.

Justice in Finances Justice is all about checks and balances, since it brings forth the consequences of financial choices. Fairness prevails as the scales tip toward balance. Evaluate your finances, seek clarity, and take responsibility for your financial circumstances while working on actionable ways to imbue more balance.

The Magick of Justice Karma doesn't judge; it brings justice. The scales of balance tip naturally, ensuring fairness in due time. Use divination tools to align with this cosmic flow, inviting harmony and Justice into every facet of your existence.

Words of Wisdom from Justice Adopt unwavering integrity in every spoken word, for within lies the power to unleash profound karma, shaping destiny's course with unwavering justice and righteous balance.

Spirit Guide—White Crane The graceful white Crane glides into your life, carrying the essence of fairness and igniting the spark of awareness. Welcome this precious gift as you navigate the intricate realm of righteousness, allowing the spirit of grace to illuminate your path and reveal the transformative power of karmic balance.

Further Indulgence Embark on a journey of inner balance. Visualize a scale, where the feather of your heart encounters the weight of your concerns. Seek harmony between reason and emotion, uncovering insights and seeking equilibrium. Welcome the images and the transformative powers of Justice.

Not everything that is faced can be changed.
But nothing can be changed until it is faced.
James A. Baldwin

12 The Hanged Man

*Hanging on a limb,
to see another way
Perspective is king,
at the end of the day
Just stuck in a moment,
in a pocket of time
Surrender by trusting,
that all will be fine*

KEYWORDS & CONCEPTS

LIGHT: letting go, mindset, unusual, perspective, pause, thinking, switch things up, surrender, juxtaposition, suspension, waiting, postponed, status quo, time-out, stasis, turn around, vulnerability, awakening

SHADOW: sacrifice, stagnation, martyrdom, stuck, clueless, strange, hesitation, inactivity, blocked, limitations, scapegoat, victim, upside down, lack of progress, hang-ups, one-sided, restriction

Scene With a thoughtful sigh, the Orangutan absentmindedly adjusts his hat, keeping the light out of his eyes. Today, he's found the perfect limb that will support his weight, while becoming the Hanged Man for a day. So he hung, as time passed, a day turned into a few as he developed such a willingness to hang suspended, for as long as it takes to resolve everything he deems wrong in his life. The more he hangs, the lighter he feels, the tightness in his chest easing, making it a bit easier to breathe and think.

As determined as he is to wait, he still hasn't let go of time, desperately clinging on to its elusive chain. Casually he looks down to check the time, when suddenly he hears a voice: "Whatcha looking at?" He flinches, realizing the source of the voice. Pausing, he looks suspiciously at the clock curled in his palm. Crinkling his nose, he fires back, "I should be asking the same of you!" The clock spins its hands wildly, retorting back, "Are you always this happy?" The Hanged Man raised an eyebrow, scoffing at the clock's sarcasm, and responded, "I'm waiting for time to pass. What's it to you?" Smugly smiling at the Orangutan at first, the clock turned straight-faced and said, "Really? Then why are you holding on to me so tight?"

The Orangutan immediately drops the clock onto the ground, as if it was a hot coal. The realization immediately struck him, smack between the eyes, as clarity came barging through the cobwebs of his mind. All this time he's felt stuck, because he refused to let anything go. Only when he heard the clock call him out did he surrender everything. Now breathing a bit easier, he climbs down from the tree. He picks up the clock, reluctantly muttering, "Um, sorry about that." Then he gingerly loops the golden chain around the tree limb, leaving a clue behind for the next Hanged Man as was purposefully left for him. As he starts walking away, he takes one last look at the inconspicuous clock and says, "Thank you; I get it now." Then he continues onward with a whole new perspective.

Hanged Man in Love Accept the transformative energy the Hanged Man brings when feeling stuck or frustrated in a relationship. Reflect on obstacles hindering growth, release what no longer serves, and open yourself to new possibilities. Embrace unconventional thinking, shift your perspective, and surrender to the power of love.

Hanged Man in Career Break free from the confines of work stagnation. Seize this precious pause to reflect, reset, and, most importantly, reassess your career path. Envision outcomes that resonate with your true calling, paving a way to a future filled with purpose and abundant fulfillment.

Hanged Man in Wellness Take a mindful pause, redirect your focus, and explore your emotions with thoughtful contemplation. This perspective will guide you toward a more healthful path. Pay attention to your body's signals, since the Hanged Man can be indicative of headaches or migraines.

Hanged Man in Finances This card brings delays and pauses, urging patience in matters of money and pending deals. Adopt a positive perspective by seeing the glass as half full, while seeking new opportunities for growth and abundance.

The Magick of the Hanged Man An activity to let go, release, and gain new perspective can be found in journaling. Take time each day to write down your thoughts, emotions, and beliefs about a particular situation or challenge. Explore different angles, question your assumptions, and seek alternative viewpoints. This practice can help you loosen attachments by shifting your perspective and opening yourself to new possibilities.

Words of Wisdom from the Hanged Man Welcome discomfort, surrender to the unknown, and unlock the transformative power of the moment, in the sacred stillness of the Hanged Man's pause.

Spirit Guide—Orangutan When the Orangutan appears, it symbolizes the beauty of embracing life's chaos. With his intelligence and laid-back nature, this spirit guide brings the gift of forward thinking. The Orangutan's gift of thought is invaluable in navigating any situation. Call on this spirit animal when needing a fresh perspective and guide through life's sticky moments.

Further Indulgence The Hanged Man embodies the essence of the Norse god Odin, inviting you to embrace divination through runes. Craft your own set, using similarly shaped unique materials such as stones, wooden discs, or glass. Mark each piece with the rune symbols, then engage in the sacred art of casting and interpreting the runes. Explore the depths of wisdom that unfold as you connect with this ancient art of divination.

*It's a moment that I'm after, a fleeting moment,
but not a frozen moment.*
Andrew Wyeth

13 Death

*The time of transition has arrived,
my soul will never die
Transformed into something
wondrous, please don't cry
In the embrace of your heart,
my essence will forever stay
The vibrations of love beyond the
grave are never far away*

KEYWORDS & CONCEPTS

LIGHT: transformation, endings, releasing, transitioning, metamorphosis, one door closes and another opens, separation by death, conclusion, stop, mortality, nothing, closure, shape-shifting

SHADOW: death, removal, loss, difficult transition, Grim Reaper, residual energy, termination, fatal, bad ending, hauntings, fatal, void, unconscious, parting, grief, attachment, decay

Scene The red stare of the Vulture matched with the snake's energy; they are trapped in this moment as a symbiotic dance teetering between death and transformation. The cold, dark stare of Death penetrates deeply, seeping into the victim's unsuspecting consciousness. Fixated on the glinting razor's edge of the scythe, the snake looks back at the Vulture and states in a flat voice, "It's time, isn't it?" The Vulture leans in close and takes a long, audible sniff as the snake recoils in horror. Death straightens up, smiling with a promise hanging on his lips. Returning his focus back to the snake, he casually asks, "Do you know the tale of the Vulture?" The snake slowly lowers his eyes, suddenly feeling uncomfortable with the direction of questioning and intense scrutiny. Greatly disappointed that the snake has never heard the tale, the Vulture shakes his head, making the little beads from his hat tinkle, mocking the sound of laughter. "Vultures appear at the moment they smell the stench of Death, resting on the precipice of pain and pleasure. I pick the bones clean of any remnants of the past life, allowing for a smooth transformation to spirit." The snake, feeling a bit braver, cautiously looks up at Death, meeting his fiery eyes, as he continues: "Forever is not meant for mortals, for their shells are fragile. Eternity belongs to the soul that has no form, forever free from its mortal constraints." The snake whispers, "But transformation feels like death." The Vulture winks and says, "It's supposed to." The snake thoughtfully tilts his face toward the warmth of the light and absently says, "Is it going to hurt?" The Vulture adjusts his grip on the scythe's hewn handle and says, "Only a little. You won't remember." The scythe comes down in one smooth motion; the only sound heard was the hum of the blade whistling through the air and then nothing . . . only silence.

Death in Love Death arrives, wielding its scythe and severing the ties holding on for dear life. In love's embrace, it signifies the descent into darkness, feeling dead inside and devoid of passion. Embrace the transformative power of death, release the past's grip, and allow the spark of rebirth, for love's resurrection awaits. With Death, you have no choice but to let go.

Death in Career Death emerges unannounced and swings the silver ax. Unexpected terminations loom, shattering the illusion of permanence or an indispensable attitude. Embrace the transformative essence of endings, navigate the shadows, and forge a new path toward unforeseen horizons.

Death in Wellness Death's haunting presence serves as a chilling reminder of life's fragility, echoing in the shadows of mortality, a stark and somber symbol that perpetually lurks in the darkness. This card may signify physical death with the correct surrounding cards, but regardless, it's always a bad omen when inquiring about health.

Death in Finances Carries a somber message of emptiness, loss of support, bankruptcies, and scarcity. It serves as a stark reminder of the importance of financial stability, urging caution and preparedness in case of unexpected challenges and endings.

The Magick of Death Honor the essence of death by creating a symbolic altar. Gather objects that represent what you wish to release. Light a black candle, speak your intentions, and let go. Watch as the flame consumes the energy symbolizing transformation. Repeat: "In death, I transform."

Words of Wisdom from Death Embrace the wisdom of Death, for within lies the metamorphosis of rebirth. Energy cannot be destroyed, only transformed, since you are pure energy!

Spirit Guide—Vulture The Vulture flies into your life, bringing the gift of death. Misunderstood and feared, it reminds us of the inevitability of change. It devours decaying and rotting flesh, leaving no remnants of the past behind, signaling the time for transformation. Death lingers in the shadows, a silent witness to the cycle and joys of living.

Further Indulgence Allow yourself the indulgence to think upon the last day your feet will touch the earth, then ask yourself, How do I want to be remembered? What you will discover is a road map leading to your life's purpose.

Life itself is but the shadow of death,
and souls departed but the shadows of the living.
Thomas Browne

14 Temperance

*In the realm of balance,
toxicity we slay
Angelic flow unravels,
negativity gives way
Temperance's alchemy,
harmonious and true
Life's blooming miracles bring
healing anew*

KEYWORDS & CONCEPTS

LIGHT: balance, healing, alchemy, peace, guardian angel, free flowing, higher self, cooperation, harmonious, health and wellness, tolerance, purity, virtue, management, integration, serenity, miracles, moderation, symmetry, back and forth, otherworldly

SHADOW: intolerance, out of touch, fallen angel, on the brink, shallow, discord, uncooperative, out of whack, imbalance, excess, off-kilter, hypochondriac, extremely one-sided, clashing, mishandled, surface level, alien

Scene One ethereal night, Temperance stands by the edge of a sacred pool guarding her gaze, cautious of the limpid water's allure, for a single rule forbids her from peering into its depths. She's served this post with honor; for a whole year and a day, she poured eternal waters from magickal vessels, in a delicate dance of balance. On her final day, she'll release the last of her vessels, brimming with enchantment upon the waiting souls below, bestowing upon them their soul's chosen wondrous human experiences. In a moment of reflection, the sounds she'll dearly miss fill her thoughts with tinkling laughter and the murmured secrets shared in whispers when miracles unfolded. Within her being, the most-cherished memories reside when a vessel pours forth symphonies of notes, their ethereal melodies ascending, unfurling a celestial rapture that tenderly caresses her eager ears.

She will not miss the echoes of bitter tears, the resounding cries of anger, or the poignant melody of heartbreak that remain when the vessels poured the weight of life's burdens upon unsuspecting souls. There have been instances when she felt the pull of temptation, a desire to glimpse into the sacred pool, but an eerie memory quickly sweeps over her, echoing words of warning: "If ever you look into the sacred waters, all that you've poured for others would be returned unto you." Those words always sent a shiver down her spine, a haunting reminder of the repercussions. Reflecting on the year gone by, she finds peace knowing that her touch brought equilibrium, intertwining the conscious and subconscious realms, revealing both the exquisite beauty of a rose and the bittersweet sting of its thorn. In the waning moments, her outstretched hand gripped the final vessel; its heaviness was noticeably burdensome today. With a furrowed brow, she ceremoniously raised it high, a mix of anticipation and trepidation. Holding her breath, she poured out the waters, yearning for the symphony of music to rise and fill the lingering stillness. In an instant, a piercing, disembodied keening fills the air, jolting her senses. Startled, she falters, nearly tumbling into the pool, her toe barely grazing the water's surface, causing a tiny ripple. Struggling to regain composure, she inadvertently glances downward, locking eyes with her own reflection, but what stares back is a distorted image of a Mushroom. Overwhelmed, she releases the vessel with a gasp—"NO!" Its contents spill, mingling with the lamentation of grief as the parched earth greedily absorbs every drop. Sinking into a heap, her gaze is fixed upon the captivating image staring back. "All this time I never knew I was a Magic Mushroom," she murmurs softly to herself. Just as the words escape her lips, a beautiful rainbow erupts overhead. Her eyes widen in disbelief at the reflection of her higher self, smiling back at her as she embraces her destiny. Astonishingly, the vessels she poured never returned to harm her; instead, a sense of perfect harmony envelops her being. With unwavering resolve, she closes her eyes and takes a deep breath, surrendering to the depths of the pool. Emerging on the other side, tears cascade down her face as she gazes into her mother's eyes, a profound sense of rebirth washing over her.

Temperance in Love This card brings balance and harmony to your relationship. Remember that fluctuations are common, but with Temperance around, she will bring equilibrium. If single, heal your heart chakra and open up your heart to make room for love.

Temperance in Career Temperance brings better management into the workplace. Also very poignant when considering careers in the healing arts, medicine, or healthcare.

Temperance in Wellness Temperance focuses on bringing moderation and harmony into your lifestyle choices, nourishing both your body and mind. Seek holistic approaches and explore practices that promote inner peace and healing.

Temperance in Finances Seek moderation and avoid extremes when it comes to spending and saving. Practice prudence in your financial decisions and consider professional advice for better money management.

The Magick of Temperance Harness the elemental power of Temperance with a tea ritual: Fill a kettle with the element of water. As it boils, visualize the transformative power of the element of fire. Add your tea to the cup, representing the healing herbs of the earth element. As you pour the fragrant brew, watch the whips of steam escaping as you inhale the element of air. Sip slowly, savoring the balance and harmony within your spirit.

Words of Wisdom from Temperance Harmony lies in the art of balance: blending opposing forces to create a symphony of serenity. Patience and moderation alchemize contentment.

Spirit Guide—Mushroom Throughout time, Mushrooms have been revered as magickal conduits, steeped in the arts of alchemy. They hold a sacred connection to the mystical art of healing, having served humanity well. These precious earthly offerings have long been revered as potent psychedelic elixirs awash in ancient wisdom carried forth in the essence of our being. When one encounters a Mushroom ring, its is seen as a divine blessing, a sign that the Fae are near.

Further Indulgence The ancient art of scrying spans across ages, calling upon seekers to delve into the depths of a reflective surface and immerse themselves in its profound mysteries. Suspended within this reflective surface are profound revelations of immense significance, patiently awaiting discovery. Let the transformative powers of magic mushrooms guide you on the sacred journey of self-discovery and spiritual exploration.

> *One psychedelic trip can make you understand more about the nature of reality than 1000s of hours of "doing" science.*
> **Robert Celner**

15 The Shadow

In the depths of your mind's echo,
I reside unseen
Whispering unkind words,
where my shadows convene
Tempting you to the dark side,
with promises I can't keep
Awaken from slumber, lest forever
in darkness you'll sleep

KEYWORDS & CONCEPTS

LIGHT: temptation, shadow work, fear, instant gratification, uncontrollable, control, desires, superstitions, dig deeper, hedonistic, cloak and dagger, sex magick, overindulgence, the unknown, playing devil's advocate, shadow self, sexuality, aware of limitations, coercion

SHADOW: devil, sabotage, fornication, addiction, insecurity, violation, exploitation, no limits, taboos, tyranny, enslavement, submission, negative attachments, servitude, constraint, obsessions, black magick, horror, panic, vices, emotional dependency, bondage, entrapment, pornography, nefarious, possessions

Scene Within the realm of inky darkness, the Black Cat's silhouette is deeper and darker than her surroundings. Such is her essence, earning her the title "the Shadow." Eyes fixed on the depths of darkness, she senses the presence of her prey, beckoning toward the scurrying sound rustling among the reeds. "The cold grips your bones; why not seek solace in the warmth of my fur?" Her voice carries into the night, drawing the sound closer. A Cheshire smile spreads across her face as two expressive eyes timidly emerge from the bull rushes. The Black Cat's voice, carried on the gentle breeze, reaches the curious ears of the mouse: "Greetings, friend; what brings you to this place, all alone?" The mouse stood on its hind legs, whiskers quivering as it sought to decipher friend or foe, weighing trust against caution with each delicate twitch of his nose. A meek voice squeaked, "I've been called to face my shadow residing within the darkness."

In the pale moonlight the cat tilted her head. Her eyes gleamed like yellow orbs as a shimmer of otherworldliness shone, casting an ethereal crimson glow atop her head. A mischievous smile twisted upon her lips as she suppressed her urge to lunge. Softening her gaze, she leaned closer and purred, "Well, that's a sign if I've ever heard one. My name's Shadow. Perhaps it was me you came to seek." The Black Cat curled her pointy tail around her body, creating a soft little nest. Purring softly, she continued, "Well, well, little mouse, this all sounds so confusing. Why don't you come over here and have a seat? We'll figure this out together." In that moment, the mouse wavered back and forth as he thought, "What a curious coincidence! Facing my shadow in the form of a cat, the embodiment of my deepest fears." Making up his mind, the mouse cautiously approached his Shadow, finding a cozy place to rest. With nefarious intentions, the Black Cat lured the mouse right where she wanted, in view of the cheese laid under the mushroom caps across the frigid stream, just deep enough for a little mouse to drown. The mouse settles in, curling into the soft fur curiously rustling up the faint smell of brimstone. Suddenly a stronger scent of cheese wafted in the air, awakening a rumbling sound of hunger from the mouse's tummy. A single raindrop descended upon his head, snapping his attention back to his Shadow. As he looked up seeking the source, his horror grew as he recognized it was the dark essence of drool that rolled off the Shadow's fang. Fear gripped his mind as he realized: it's a trap. At the same time, the Black Cat sensed a shift, feeling fear's rapid heartbeat hammering against her midnight fur. In a sudden burst of ingenuity, the mouse's instincts propelled him into action, feigning his way toward the water, then deftly swerving at the edge, eluding the clutches of his Shadow by vanishing safely into the reeds.

Shadow in Love The Shadow's grip in love weaves a web of exploitation, fueled by control and bondage. Beware of the seductive allure that masks manipulation. Find emancipation and break free from these chains, reclaiming your power, and quell the fear of intimacy.

Shadow in Career Manifests as entrapment and exploitation. Beware of toxic work environments and power dynamics that strip away your autonomy. Avoid the guilt trips and manipulation traps of superiors. Trust your instincts.

Shadow in Wellness Fear, the ultimate restraint, obscures true living, ensnaring minds in shadows. This card exposes the impact of mental illness and sexual abuse, urging caution.

Shadow in Finances Debt and addiction may ensnare, trapping you in a cycle of dependency. Break free by facing your financial demons. Adopt an attitude of discipline and seek salvation from toxic money patterns. Beware of self-destructive behaviors such as overspending and missed payments, which exacerbate debt.

The Magick of the Shadow Within the depths of the Shadow lies the portal to transformation and self-awareness. Absorb your darkest aspects; confront your fears and integrate them into your being. Through shadow work, harness the soul's wisdom, unlocking profound healing and inner peace.

Words of Wisdom from the Shadow In life, two forces prevail: love and fear. Embrace love, for it triumphs over fear, unlocking the power to conquer all.

Spirit Guide—Black Cat Embrace the enigmatic presence of the Black Cat, a familiar to witches and a symbol of mystery. Peer into your Shadow, discover hidden truths, and embark on a journey, using the healing power of shadow work. Allow the Black Cat to guide you through the darkness and illuminate your path to self-discovery.

Further Indulgence Embrace the allure of the shadows, exploring the depths of your desires and fears. Engage in a creative ritual of sexual expression, allowing your innermost passion and vulnerabilities to surface, discovering the power of sexual energy.

*Those who were afraid of the dark and always refused
to throw themselves inside it never got to see and feel how beautiful it is,
to meet and greet one's own demons.*
Akshay Vasu

16 The Tower

*Life's moving along, and suddenly
with no guarantee
Angry skies unleash a bolt,
making a big catastrophe
Frail foundations crumble, burdened
by sorrow's weight
As the universe makes room,
by creating a clean slate*

KEYWORDS & CONCEPTS

LIGHT: rebuilding, warning, orgasmic, falling, eureka, drastic change, structures, damage, coming apart, injury, setback, harm, incident, trouble, foreshadowing, mishap, harbinger, breakthrough, cracks in the foundation, wake-up call, unstable, purification

SHADOW: fire, catastrophe, breakdown, destruction, ruin, volatile, downfall, demolition, chaos, obliteration, decimation, explosive, sudden and unexpected, breaking apart, disaster, collapse, accidents, faulty foundation, upheaval, resistant to change

Scene On a bright, clear, ordinary day in Butterfly Meadows, a faraway rumble deeply penetrates the peace, followed by a clap of thunder. This warning was way too close, as the sound is felt reverberating throughout the Tower, shaking it right down to its core. Over time, the Tower's structural integrity started failing, since it had weathered many storms. First to appear was a hairline fracture right at the base by the door. As years rolled by, the neglected crack quickly became a structural hazard, but nothing that a few strategically placed topiaries couldn't fix, just to keep up the facade. After that last tremor, the Fox became very concerned, feeling that something was

off. He called out to his friend, "Hey, Hare, why don't you come outside and give me a hand? I need to check the perimeter of the Tower." The Hare, watching his favorite show and not wanting to be disturbed, called back to his friend, "Nah, go ahead. I'm at the best part when they give out the final carrot." The Fox rolled his eyes in the hare's direction, shook his head, and set out to give things a quick once-over.

Upon exiting the door, he immediately turns around and witnesses the foundation crack reaching its ugly hand up toward the angry sky. Out of the blue, a flash of white-hot lightning slices through the night air, reaching down to hit the existing crack as if it was target practice. The Fox freezes as everything starts crumbling before his very eyes. The Tower began to give way and split in two. Shaking himself out of the frozen shock, the Fox finds his voice and screams in horror. Feeling helpless, he can do nothing to stop this Tower moment from happening as he witnesses the disaster unfold. He continued desperately screaming over the roar of chaos until his voice was raw: "You should have listened to the warnings! You should have gotten out! Hare! Do you hear me? HARE!" He tearfully watched as orange flames engulfed the windows, the same windows that only five minutes earlier looked onto the beautiful woods. Now he watched as his friend desperately jumped from one of them.

The catastrophe continued to rain down ruination upon the earth. Fire leapt from the pits of hell, licking flames upward and singeing everything its path, leaving its mark. Running over to the prone body of his friend, the Fox exhales when he gets close enough to see his friend is still breathing. Although he made it out alive, he didn't make it out unscathed, for none escape the Tower untouched.

The Tower in Love The Tower stands as a formidable symbol of upheaval. As the foundation crumbles, release the rubble of a broken connection. Embrace the lessons learned. Remember you can't hold on to someone who doesn't want to be held.

The Tower in Career The Tower's disruptive presence in the workplace signifies a sudden shake-up and unexpected downfall of established order. Welcome chaos as an opportunity to reduce to ash what stands in the way of a fulfilling career. A new path will emerge, leading you to greater heights and untapped potential.

The Tower in Wellness The Tower shows up in the form of stubbornness. Focus on flexibility by staying limber. The shape of the Tower is very phallic, since it can represent the male reproductive system or the rigidity of the spine when inquiring about health.

The Tower in Finances The Tower forewarns of a financial crisis, real estate bubbles imploding, markets crashing, or insurmountable rising costs. Take precautions to avoid financial ruin: stay informed, heed financial warnings.

The Magick of the Tower Beware of the cracks, for they foretell upheaval. From small tremors to crumbling structures, heed the warnings and take action. By addressing the fractures, you can prevent complete breaks and repair the foundation, rebuilding the Tower even stronger.

Words of Wisdom from the Tower As the Tower crumbles, embrace the fall, for it will reveal hidden strength within. Amid the rubble, seeds of resilience take root, paving the way for renewal. From the ashes of destruction, rise higher, resurrected with unwavering determination and an indomitable spirit. Let the Tower's collapse be the catalyst for your rebirth; this is your second chance.

Spirit of the Tower The old and ancient Tower stands the test of time, proud and indestructible until it falls to its knees in ruin, humbled by an unstoppable force of nature. The Tower offers a gift of warning; that powerful instinct tells you something is not quite right. It is those quiet whispers you need to hear the loudest, for they are the first warnings.

Further Indulgence Think back to the Tower moments of your life, defining times that rocked your world and shattered your foundation. Times when you felt so broken, wishing that the ground would crack open and swallow you whole. But remember, it's through your darkest nights that your light shines brightest.

Life delivered me a catastrophe, but I found a richness of soul.
Michael J. Fox

17 The Star

Against the dark canvas of the heavens shines a big, bright star
Guiding travelers and inspiring lovers, a celestial light from afar
A beacon of hope granting wishes, believing dreams come true
Careful what you wish for, because it finds its way back to you

KEYWORDS & CONCEPTS

LIGHT: beliefs, aspirations, divine guidance, constellations, overview, renewal, culmination, universe, wishes, expansive, fame, hope, cosmic energy, visualization, pure energy, goals, science, astrology, systems, freedom, vision, enlightenment, macrocosmos, validation, discovery, future, improvement, aspirations, alignment, superconscious

SHADOW: dishonor, disillusionment, microcosmos, hopeless, uninspired, pseudoscience, blindness, unconventional, disbelief, aimless direction, exposure, spiritual blocks, misalignment, pessimism, unclear, infamy

Scene A Star burst in the night sky, shining so bright it briefly outshone the moon. The cascade of starlight gently floats downward, touching the earth, and materializing into a Unicorn. Against the inky sky the woodland creatures witnessed a blaze of light and came running into the clearing of daisies. They stood shoulder to shoulder in awe, before the presence of the most beautiful creature, for they've never seen such a mythical beast before. The town mayor cautiously approached the fabled creature by landing on a nearby twig. The Unicorn swished its long, milky tail, acknowledging the mayor's presence. The mayor calmly regarded the Unicorn in the most curious manner. Not knowing how to begin, he swallowed visibly and said, "Welcome, celestial being, on behalf of myself and the townsfolk here! We offer you thanks and hospitality for honoring us with your light this eve." The Unicorn shook its long mane as twinkles of starlight fell from his silky tresses. Scanning all who had gathered, his icy-blue eyes rested back on the mayor. "My name is Star. I've come from a place very far from your timeline. I have visited this place you call Earth once before, and, I see, your history remembers me well." The mayor nervously added, "Yes, we've heard the stories and seen the likeness of your kind in books. But until this very moment we could only believe of your existence."

Star tossed his glorious mane once again and turned to address the crowd, "I come bringing inspiration. A breath of fresh air that ignites the spark into action and turns into an inferno of creation. Remember this night, for I will be your muse. Whenever you have need, just look to the heavens and find me there, shining down blessings upon you." With that said, and the celestial event complete, Star leapt toward the sky, pushing upward with his powerful legs and flying higher and higher until he disappeared among the twinkling stars. The townsfolk were in awe, murmuring with excitement to have received such a gift, so grateful that they followed that falling Star one fateful night.

Star in Love In matters of the heart, the Star brings celestial blessings. It signifies the alignment of cosmic forces that guide your relationship's fate. If you're in a relationship, take this as a sign that your union is written in the stars. For those seeking love, the Star beckons you to make a wish upon its radiant presence, for the universe is listening and ready to manifest your heart's desires.

Star in Career Success shines upon your career path. Recognition, rewards, and promotions await as you shine as a Star employee. Accept the abundant blessings of the Star and allow it to be your guide on your stellar journey.

Star in Wellness There's always hope. The Star is a positive card, bringing improvement to any ailment or situation. This card instills an attitude of feeling comfortable in one's own skin. The Star is the embodiment of health and happiness, and everything wishes are made of.

Star in Finances The Star brings improvement and success to any business or financial venture. A great card to see when asking about finances.

The Magick of the Star The Star brings the magick of Wishcraft, the opportunity to manifest what you desire. So make a wish!

Words of Wisdom from the Star Live out your biggest dreams by writing and starring in your own story.

Spirit Guide—Unicorn This mythical Unicorn, a symbol of magick and grace, emerges as your guide. It brings the gift of divine inspiration and shines starlight on the unique brilliance that lies within you. In its divine presence, you're reminded of your limitless potential, transcending the ordinary and embracing the extraordinary. Allow the Unicorn to ignite the spark of greatness, guiding your soul on a profound journey of self-actualization. Welcome the pure energy to fuel your wildest dreams and manifest them into reality. Together, you become a radiant force, creating enchantment in every step of your sacred path. Remember, wishes do come true when the Unicorn graces your life.

Further Indulgence Bathed in celestial light, the Star illuminates your astrological chart, guiding you toward your true purpose. Embrace the cosmic energy, aligned with your cosmic blueprint, and shine brightly as the unique constellation that you are. A great starting point can be to discover your Sun, Moon, and Ascendant signs in astrology. This information provides great insight, helping you celebrate your strengths while working on your weaknesses.

Moonlight drowns out all but the brightest stars.
J. R. R. Tolkien, Lord of the Rings

18 The Moon

*Seeding my dreams with lovers,
wispy ghosts of the past
Full moon toying with my emotions,
making feelings last
With karmic relationships I still
struggle, of lives left behind
A figment of my imagination?
Or a remnant left in the mind?*

KEYWORDS & CONCEPTS

LIGHT: intuition, feminine energy, mystery, dreams, fluctuations, the crone, lunar cycles, influence, past lives, imagination, the past, ebb and flow, meditation, inner realms, tidal pull, reflection, hidden truths, enchantment, natural cycles, subconscious

SHADOW: myopic, confusion, deception, deep subconscious, misunderstandings, irrational, unknown, disenchantment, emotional turbulence, compelled, regression, waning, illusion, maya, blocked intuition, hidden desire, paranoia

Scene Enshrined in the Moon, the spirit of the She-wolf pulsates with enchantment, as she quietly watches over the dreamy world. She sends shafts of glowing beams into the night's sky, letting her soft glow filter down, influencing the dreams of the ones sleeping below. As the tides shift, a Crayfish instinctually feels the pull into the mysterious light. This phenomenon is remarkably irresistible to the Crayfish as he makes his way to the surface, where hidden things come to light. Climbing onto a rock, he basks in her glow as he waits, for what, he does not know, but the anticipation is becoming

too great as raw emotions make his claws scissor in the air, instinctively trying to grasp the source of mystique.

Suddenly a low howl echoes throughout the land. The eerie sound makes the antennas on the Crayfish stand at attention, as bravery wanes and fear starts to creep in under his hard shell. Confused, desperately looking for the source of the sound, his eyes settle on an image in the center of the Moon, making eye contact with the most beautiful creature he's ever seen. "Goodnight, Crayfish, what brings you out this full moon?" Shocked, the Crayfish sucks in his breath and says, "It was the glow of your light that called out to me." The Moon smiled knowingly, as the light danced in her eyes. "That's what I call intuition, that gut feeling continuously moving through you, coaxing you in the direction of your soul's path." The Crayfish scratches his head with his pincer, trying to grasp the concept, although quickly the confusion turns into concern. Frowning, he starts to worry, wondering where his soul's path is leading to. Every day is pretty much the same for him: hide, look for food, eat, and sleep. The Moon tunes into his thoughts, chuckling softly at the perplexed look on the Crayfish's face. Hearing the laughter, the Crayfish looks up. "Hey, Moon, how did you know what I was thinking?" The She-wolf slowly nods and answers, "I'm psychic. I use my intuition, you know, as you do when you sense danger. You instinctively know to swish your tail, swimming backward quickly fleeing from threats." The Crayfish nods back, satisfied with the newfound knowledge, now understanding much more than before. He looks back at the gorgeous Moon a final time before slipping into the cool, fresh waters welcoming him home. Time for sleep, for tomorrow he's determined to find his soul's path too. For he must have one if he's to embrace this ever-changing world.

Moon in Love The enigmatic Moon reveals the intertwining threads of the past, illuminating the echoes of a karmic relationship that still has tidal pulls on your heart. Seek authenticity and leave the ghosts of the past behind for any semblance of future happiness. In a current relationship, beware of deception and illusions by staying vigilant as the moonlight casts many gradient shadows of the truth.

Moon in Career The Moon reveals misunderstandings in the workplace. Address them promptly to prevent things festering and escalating into significant issues. When seeking employment, the Moon warns of unfavorable outcomes. Stay vigilant for deceptions and navigate with caution in your workplace.

Moon in Wellness Beware of hidden health issues, since the Moon shines light on the cycles of the female reproductive system. Symbolizing the crone years, it emphasizes the wisdom and inner power as the wise blood is now held within.

Moon in Finances Brings uncertainty and fluctuations in financial matters. Beware of hidden pitfalls and deceptive opportunities. Trust your intuition and seek clarity in financial decisions. Say abreast and adapt to the changing tides of the financial landscape.

The Magick of the Moon Incorporate moon phases for timing spells or intentions, and watch the magick unfold.

Words of Wisdom from the Moon As you behold me in the vastness of the night sky, I am ever present, watching over you on your journey. My luminous rays carry whispers of love and understanding, so confide in me your secrets and share your sorrows. I will collect your tears and embrace them within my radiant glow.
  With infinite celestial affection,
  The Moon

Further Indulgence Indulge in the Moon's cycle and observe her enchantment for 28 days. Bask in her ethereal presence, whether seen or unseen, and feel her energy. Journal, recording dates, moon phases, emotions, and experiences. Discover the ebb and flow of your psyche through her lunar embrace.

Spirit Guide—Crayfish As a creature of water and dreams, the Crayfish brings the gift of regeneration. Like the Moon's reflection, it swims backward into the past, urging us to embrace introspection. Its resilience in its ability to take a beating and regrow lost limbs teaches us to adapt and renew. Follow the Crayfish's guidance and dive deep into the present moment. Accept the moon's healing embrace by transmuting past pain.

Further Indulgence Once a month, when the Moon is full, meditate on something you seek clarity on. Harness the power of the moon to illuminate the truth, helping you see through the illusion. This will allow you to take back control of your emotions by focusing on the good, instead of creating comforting stories in your head or imagining the worst. Time to get real.

> *If someday the moon calls you by your name, don't be surprised,*
> *because every night I tell her about you.*
> **Shahrazad al-Khalij**

19 The Sun

*Blissful sunshine beaming,
joy and happiness I bestow
Living life in the moment,
making everything thrive and grow
With the gift of transparency,
I bring clarity and see right through
The Sun illuminates shadowy lies,
granting truthfulness out
of the blue*

KEYWORDS & CONCEPTS

LIGHT: happiness, prosperity, growth, vitality, masculine energy, transparency, the present, success, breakthrough, happy child, wholeness, accolades, truth, reality, yes, joy, enjoyment, accomplishments, optimism, good omens, summer, conscious

SHADOW: ungrateful, shade, blame, unhappiness, decline, misfortune, dullness, difficulty in seeing the good, unappreciative, taken for granted, vagueness, fizzling out, convoluted

Scene Southerly the Sun moves across the midday sky, turning everything into spun gold. The Sunflower looks over the fields, feeling the warmth of the Sun radiating on her face as she basks in his glorious rays. The Hobbyhorse turns toward the Sunflower and asks, "What does it feel like to be real?" The Sunflower swivels her head toward the voice and replies, "To feel the Sun upon your face." Demonstrating this feat, the Sunflower tilts her face toward the light. The Hobbyhorse surprisingly notices that the darker-colored parts of him are definitely warmer—she has a point. Looking into her beautiful face, the Hobbyhorse gives her a big smile. The Sunflower flashes back a

dazzler of her own, as she continues, "And to bring joy and spread happiness." The Hobbyhorse can barely contain his excitement, shouting and rocking back and forth, "Yes! YES! I do loads of that!" The Sunflower nods her head, and her petals wave in enthusiasm, mimicking the rhythmic movements of the wooden horse. At last she declares with gusto, "It's to feel alive!"

The Hobbyhorse, crestfallen, quickly turns away, suddenly becoming very still. Seeing this, the Sunflower raises herself to full height, channeling the vitality of the Sun's rays, and states, "See all my children at your feet? I follow the Sun to feel his warmth on my face. I bring joy to all that lay eyes upon me, for I am the embodiment of the Sun." The Hobbyhorse quietly listened but felt even worse. Immediately the Sunflower noticed another shift in energy, and, shining even brighter, she declares, "You, too, are alive! Once you were a living tree, rooted deep in the ground. Then you were cut down and shaped lovingly into a form that brings joy and happiness to the living. You were made with love, and the energy remains within, for energy cannot be destroyed; it only changes forms. You are part of the tree, as my children are a part of me." And with that, the Sunflower reached down and affixed a couple of sunflowers to the Hobbyhorse's mane. It was in that very moment the Hobbyhorse felt so seen and real!

Sun in Love In the realm of love, the Sun shines its radiant light on the bonds of friendship. Friendships form the bedrock of relationships, fostering trust and deep connection. This card heralds a bright future, promising joy with the potential for a happy and fulfilling relationship.

Sun in Career Time to shine! Trust that you're the right person for that job. Welcome the "YES!" card into your life. Say yes to new opportunities and stop standing in your own way. Capture the moment. Unleash your brilliance and pursue your path of happiness.

Sun in Wellness Sun therapy fills your body with sunshine and free vitamin D, recharging your body and illuminating your spirit. Channel the Sun's healing power; radiate its energy outward, sharing your sunshine with others. Nourish yourself with sunflower seeds to keep worries at bay and welcome the vitality of the Sun's medicine into your body.

Sun in Finances Financial abundance is within reach. Welcome new opportunities and embrace bold actions. The Sun shines a light on prosperity and success. Be confident, trust your abilities, and let your financial endeavors bask in the warmth of the Sun's blessings.

The Magick of the Sun Harness the Sun's divine energy through solar magick. Charge a gold amulet in sunlight to evoke the Sun God's healing power. Wear it as a talisman, renewing its energy regularly. Remember that the Sun is a powerful healer.

Words of Wisdom from the Sun Rise each day with renewed possibilities. Embrace your inner radiance, ignite passion, and inspire others. Bask in your brilliance, for within you burns the eternal flame of the present moment.
    With radiant blessings,
    The Sun

Spirit of the Sunflower The Sunflower is a beacon of joy and resilience, mirroring the qualities of the Sun. Its vibrant petals radiate happiness, while its seeds nourish growth and ensure the legacy of future tomorrows. Let the spirit of the Sunflower guide you, infusing your soul with the pure energy of sunshine filtering its rays of fulfillment into all aspects of your life.

Further Indulgence On a sunny day, stand in the sunlight and welcome its healing rays into your body. Allow the golden light to flow from your crown to your feet, connecting the radiant light to the core of Mother Earth. This beautiful practice recharges, grounds, and protects, nurturing your balance and vitality.

A sunflower field is like a sky with a thousand suns.
    Corina Abulahm-Negura

20 Judgement

*A part of me has vanished,
lost in the depths of time
Awaiting the call of Judgement,
a fate I can't define
I ask to be awakened and embrace
a true rebirth
Returned to life again, feel my feet
upon the earth*

KEYWORDS & CONCEPTS

LIGHT: rebirth, regeneration, retrospective, new outlook on life, soul's purpose, self-assessment, redemption, reviewing past mistakes, forgiveness, accountability, reincarnation, awakening, revival, renewal, resurrection

SHADOW: judgement, scrutiny, criticism, unforgiving, consequences, not learning from your past mistakes, second-guessing yourself, disappointed with life so far, defeated, regrets, guilt, torment, feeling judged, resistant to change, denial

Scene On a foggy night, the starkly visible Arctic Fox feels exposed against a backdrop of darkness. He's been summoned by the magistrate, who asked him here on this dark night of his soul. The Arctic Fox arrived on time, his eyes quickly adjusting to the thickness of the fog rolling in, as he inconspicuously looked around at the tombs of the ones worthy of eternal rest. Time has not been so kind to the weathered stones, since he can no longer make out the names of the righteous. The magistrate caws loudly, snapping back the attention of the Arctic Fox to the crow's beak as he begins to speak, "I am the magistrate of this place. They call me Judgement." Instantaneously the Arctic Fox's knees start to tremble in fear; he feels trapped in this circumstance and thinks, "This can't be good."

The magistrate's beak is moving. "I've called upon you this eve, to pass judgement. But before I do, I'll give you one final warning . . . stop going through the motions, embrace all of life's moments, and live each day to the fullest." Paralyzed, the Arctic Fox hears the message loud and clear, very grateful for a second chance, because this could've gone really, really bad. Judgement tilts his head, staring down his beak at the poor soul, with interest in his beady little crow's eye. As he continues to speak, the amusement in his voice ripples off the Fox's body, stirring the creature's hairs and making them stand on end. "As long as you go through this lifetime conscious of your actions, always striving for the highest good in your deeds, you will have no reason to fear your day of Judgement. Yes, you will make mistakes. But if you learn, they won't be held against you." Judgement stretches out a midnight wing, granting the Fox's leave. The Arctic Fox promptly catches his drift. Feeling his feet suddenly come to life, he leaps out of there in a blink of an eye, muttering under his breath, "Damn, that was close!"

Judgement in Love If in a relationship, there is a vein of judgment that impedes having a healthful balanced romance. If single, especially after a prolonged period, be mindful of being too picky and judgmental toward others. Seek openness and release judgment to create meaningful connections.

Judgement in Career Be mindful of overly critical colleagues; their criticism often reflects their own mental and emotional state. Stay confident in your own abilities, for true confidence is silent when insecurities tend to be loud.

Judgement in Wellness When you feel the weight of judgment from others, remember that their opinions don't define your worth. Look inward and adopt self-acceptance. Nurture your soul by practicing self-care, mindfulness, and visualization. Release the burden of judgment and reclaim your inner peace.

Judgement in Finances Feeling disappointed by your finances? Don't pass judgment yet. Assess the whole picture and seek guidance for a clearer perspective.

The Magick of Judgement Mirror work: stand before a mirror, look into your eyes, and say,
> *I am worthy, I am enough, and I release the judgments of others.*
> *I embrace my authentic self and find strength in my own validation.*
> *I am unaffected by their opinions. I am free.*

Feel the words surge through you as you let go of external judgments and reclaim your power.

Words of Wisdom from Judgement What we judge in others is the part of ourselves we hate the most.

Spirit Guides—Arctic Fox The Arctic Fox, a wise spirit guide, brings the gift of camouflage and observation. Learn to inconspicuously blend in with others, gathering intel unnoticed while melding into your surroundings. Being a master of invisibility and keen instincts will alert you to danger and keep you safe from harm.

Further Indulgence Embrace self-acceptance and shed Judgement's weight. Your worth isn't defined by other opinions. Nurture your inner voice; reject criticism. Reflect, grow, and radiate in authenticity. Relish in the realness of you, amid this watered-down, accepted version of reality. Be unapologetically yourself, honoring your true essence.

When you judge others, you do not define them; you define yourself.
Earl Nightingale

21 The World

*End with the World back to the Fool;
knowledge became my wealth
A whole revolution is now complete,
as I spiral back into myself
I've learned many lessons in life,
finding myself along the way
Until I reach the end of the road,
I'll keep showing up every day*

KEYWORDS & CONCEPTS

LIGHT: completion, universe, integration, availability, fulfillment, transcendence, wholeness, showing up, all in, cosmic consciousness, togetherness, worldly, encompassing, openness, autonomy, physical experiences, achievement, final outcome, earth, reconciliation, completion of a full rotation

SHADOW: commercialism, complexities, enclosure, unrealized goals, limitations, unsupportive, uninvolved, estrangement, humanism, encircled, end of the road, lack of closure, unfilled potential, lack of integration, feeling trapped, recurring issues, mundaneness

Scene The Koala Bear tenderly cradles the World in the palm of her hand, as she lovingly presses her cheek against the earth's cool surface, soothing the souls encased within. From time to time she gazes into the World, looking in on humanity, keeping tabs to see how they're progressing. After a while her eyes magnetically get drawn into the swirls of fluffy clouds, instantly mesmerized and getting lost in her own thoughts. Feeling a bit of melancholy, she whispers quietly to the World, "If only you knew how precious life is; the

ability to sense and experience all things felt deeply in your corporeal form is truly the greatest gift of your soul."

The Koala Bear breaks out of her trance, longingly wondering if they heard, or if maybe they chose to ignore the voice in the wind. Now, she exists on the outside looking in, watching the scenes unfold like a movie, living vicariously only through memories of the Fool. She sighs and speaks to herself, "If only they knew how precious it is to be alive, they'd never take life for granted again." The excitement becomes palatable, because today is the day she gets the sacred privilege of hugging the World, a reward bestowed for the successful completion of the journey of her soul. Smiling, the Koala holds the World in a brief embrace, feeling closer to her experiences once more. As half the World slumbers beneath her furry blanket of darkness, she squeezes her eyes, savoring the experience as she feels alive again.

World in Love The World signifies completion, unity, and wholeness, so celebrate your relationship as you move through toward fulfillment of love's odyssey. For those single, seek closure and release the lovers of the past. Let go of any lingering questions and "What ifs" and embrace the boundless possibilities that love has in store for you.

World in Career This card brings about an organic ending, after a successful completion of a project or workplace experience. The end has come, and it's time to move on to something new that's even bigger and better. The World is your oyster, waiting for you to explore and conquer.

World in Wellness Expand your horizons by exploring a new wellness practice and finding what truly resonates with you. Step into a state of wholeness and vibrant vitality when aligning with the energy of the World. When it comes to a health condition, this card signifies a natural completion and brings closure to a chapter.

World in Finances Achieve financial fulfillment by embracing a global perspective. Expand your financial horizons, explore new worlds, and seek investment diversification. The World card signifies completion and success in business matters.

The Magick of the World Tap into the cosmic energy of the World through rituals that symbolize completion and manifestation. Create a sacred space, meditate, and visualize your goals coming into fruition. Allow the interconnectedness of the universe by harnessing its transformative powers to manifest your earthly desires.

Words of Wisdom from the World The World turns in perfect harmony. Every experience in your life has purpose. Embrace your inner microcosmos, for within it lies the power to shape your reality. You are all little worlds in and of yourself, a unique entity that contributes to the vastness of the whole universe. Trust in yourself and your connection to the grand tapestry of existence.

Spirit Guide—Koala Bear The Koala comes into your world, letting you know it's time to chill out, slow down, and enjoy every moment. Munching on those eucalyptus leaves all day brings on a euphoric effect, flooding the Koala with perpetual tranquility balancing both her inner and outer worlds.

Further Indulgence The World is the embodiment of the subconscious, the conscious, and the superconscious, allowing the soul to fully express itself in this earthy classroom and to experience and physically express itself completely in incarnate form. Manifestation exercise: Start by visualizing something small but specific that you would like to physically appear in your life. An example would be a red button. Be on the lookout for a red button. Once this object has manifested, challenge yourself with progressively harder and more-specific manifestations.

The world you see outside you will always be a
reflection of what you have inside you.
Cory Booker

The Minor Arcana

The 56 Minor cards reflect daily mundane occurrences and experiences of living life. They offer valuable situational insight by providing guidance on how to proceed, to ensure a favorable outcome. The Minors are composed of suits: Wands, Cups, Swords, and Pentacles. Each suit contains an ace through ten and the Court Cards, comprising a Page, Knight, Queen, and King, representing various people and mundane events that you have influence over.

THE SUIT OF WANDS

The suit of Wands primarily carries an active masculine energy with themes of ideas, action, desires, careers, initiative, energy, projects, growth, passion, creativity, inspiration, ambitions, movement, and expansion.

THE SUIT OF CUPS

The suit of cups primarily carries a passive feminine energy, with the themes of emotions, reflection, intuition and psychic abilities, relationships, creativity, imagination, love, dreams, visualization, the subconscious, feelings, and spirit.

THE SUIT OF SWORDS

The suit of swords primarily carries an active masculine energy, with the themes of slicing and cutting, challenges, discussions, removals, struggles, logic, communication, intelligence, conflicts, decisions, thoughts, and the power of the mind.

THE SUIT OF PENTACLES

The suit of pentacles primarily carries a passive feminine energy, with the themes of money, manifestation, work, skills, stability, resources, tangible things, material life, security, finances, health, validation, and reaping what you sow.

Ace of Wands

*Learning as you go along,
trying to find some motivation
Inspiration blazing, fired up and
yearning for stimulation
A new day commences, the moment
you open your eyes
For a chance to be great again,
take your shot at the prize*

KEYWORDS & CONCEPTS

LIGHT: inspiration, passion, new idea, energy, enthusiasm, initiative, creative potential, new opportunity, self-growth, spark of creativity, fire element, the Beginning, intimacy, magick wand, initial thought, motivation, new situation, exclamation, spontaneity

SHADOW: meaningless, idleness, uninspired, creative block, procrastination, lacking originality, burnout, anger, overlooked, unimaginative, impotence, inflated ego, impatient, restless

Scene The Ace of Wands shoots out beside a glorious sunflower, proudly shining and ready to take on the world. The light of warm hues forms a swath across the sky, immersing the wand in brilliance, helping it grow straight and true, hidden among the plethora of sunflowers in plain sight of the world.

One beautiful, lazy, hazy summer's day, you decided to go out for a walk to break up the monotony of life's routine, knowing that fresh air and time in nature does good for the soul. A ways into your journey, a feeling comes over you. You hesitate to take the next step, instead turning your head toward

the source of energy you feel. Hidden in a field of sunflowers, you see something different: something tall and shiny is sticking out of the patch. Curiosity clutches your heart as you cautiously make your way through the field for a closer look. The brilliance immediately hits your eyes, causing you to squint as you raise a hand to shield your view. Your mouth drops, since you can't believe your eyes! It looks like a scene right out of a fairy tale; so stunning, it momentarily leaves you breathless. Waves of energy emit from the wand, as the magick comes to life right before your very eyes. The leaves on the wand transfigure into delightful butterflies, while seeds of inspiration explode, shooting far and wide into the world. You immediately leap into action, hands flailing and wildly grasping at the air in hopes of catching a seed of your very own. Tightly squeezing your palm, you feel a treasure trapped within. Closing your eyes and tilting your head toward the Ace of Wands, you whisper, "Thank you."

You never knew that when you set out today, your life would change. This was exactly what you needed, to find this glorious seed of inspiration. You hurry home, excited to plant the seeds of tomorrow.

Ace of Wands in Love This Ace ignites the flames of passion and connection, turning a tiny spark into a raging inferno of love. Be open to new romantic possibilities or rekindling a past flame. There are sparks of passion, intimacy, attraction, sexual arousal, and connection, as well as a probability for love at first sight when the Ace of Wands is around.

Ace of Wands in Career Seedlings of a new idea begin to form, bringing about a new opportunity. Something will manifest out of thin air, so be on the lookout for a tiny spark that has the potential to ignite and turn into a mighty career. Surround yourself with supportive allies who believe in your idea during this most crucial beginning.

Ace of Wands in Wellness A new solution emerges to alleviate any concerns you may have. Pay attention to signs guiding you toward creative ways to find release.

Ace of Wands in Finances This card brings a new financial opportunity. Grasp this initial offering, seeing it all the way through to fruition.

The Magick of the Ace of Wands Inspiration comes blazing forth, bringing passion, initiating a new beginning. Light a red candle, symbolizing passion and creativity. Meditate on your goals; visualize them coming to life. Write down your intentions and place them near the candle. Feel the intense energy of inspiration and safely burn the paper, releasing your intentions into the universe.

Words of Wisdom from the Ace of Wands Ignite the divine spark of the Ace of Wands. Unleash your creative power to shape the universe within and around you.

Spirit of the Sunflower The Sunflower constantly tilts its face toward sunlight, forever turning its back on darkness. Its inspiration runs though its stalk, making it grow tall and prouder than the rest of the flowers, spreading its seeds across the land and ensuring future generations.

Who knows what may lie around the next corner?
There may be a window somewhere ahead. It may look out
on a field of sunflowers.
Joe Hill

Two of Wands

Standing at the edge of possibility,
waiting for my time to come
Looking for my turn to shine and
bask in the warmth of the sun
Up ahead at the next junction of life,
tough choices must be made
The greatest gift is to live fully
before disappearing into the fade

KEYWORDS & CONCEPTS

LIGHT: choice to be made, pioneer, planning, partnership, next steps, period of waiting, compromise, contemplation, vision, potential, big picture, deciding, trailblazer, strategy, discovery

SHADOW: indecision, holding back, lack of direction, wasting time, winging it, refusing to give an inch, putting no thought into it, eager to get moving, stalling, second-guessing, lacking vision, missed opportunity

Scene Holding a world of possibility in the palm of his hand, the little Mouse projects his aspirations forth into the world. As he moves around, bouncing from foot to foot, he can hardly contain himself. His seed of inspiration sowed into his mind has sprouted, with new and exciting ideas. Now standing on the precipice between worlds, a place where energy hangs with a pregnant breath in between being and nonbeing, where anything and everything is possible in that moment. Holding on tightly to one of the wands, he firmly establishes his neutrality as he casts his line of sight far and

wide, seeing all angles while he formulates a master plan. The Mouse becomes aware of the passage of time. His joints scream with fatigue, since he hasn't moved a muscle for some time; looking up, he sees the glow of the full moon ascending toward her zenith.

Just on the verge of thrusting the globe forth between the portal created by boundary of the Two of Wands, he immediately stops and second-guesses himself. Thoughts of failure fill his vision like spiderwebs ensnaring his dreams, so he intently pauses once again, listening and waiting for a sign. Fear settles into the Mouse's heart, stealing the breathless kiss of inspiration the muse had given him. Closing his eyes, he draws a breath and lets out a sigh. Upon opening his eyes, he witnesses the rapid spinning of the globe. Mesmerized by the velocity of the spin, everything becomes a blur. He rapidly blinks in hopes of slowing the globe. To no avail, the World spins faster and faster, emitting a high-pitched sound forming whispers of words barely audible: "If you stay, you will become a hazard to yourself, and your own worst enemy. So blaze a path forward, for you are the first of your kind to venture this far out. As you now stand at the edge of existence, I wait. The next move is yours." The Mouse takes a deep, cleansing breath and lays his hand upon his heart to keep the words safe, knowing that this is the sign he has been waiting for. Now, full of confidence, he thrusts the World forth between the Two of Wands, as his body automatically follows through. Upon opening his eyes, he exclaims, "Wow! Where am I?"

Two of Wands in Love In matters of love, the Two of Wands invites contemplation. Step back, assess your feelings, and seek new ways to explore them. Embrace the unknown and be open to new partners or partnerships that ignite your passion and expand your love bubble.

Two of Wands in Career Life should not be consumed by climbing proverbial ladders or breaking glass ceilings. Finding the sweet spot of a healthful work-life balance is key to a rewarding career. This is a critical time for strategic planning to move you into alignment with your dreams.

Two of Wands in Wellness Finding balance in your wellness goals is paramount. Instead of overwhelming yourself, focus on taking one step at time toward a healthful habit. Each intentional choice and small change leads to a healthy, balanced life. Trust your instincts and consider exploring alternative therapies for treatment that align with your needs.

Two of Wands in Finances Exercise caution when introducing new elements to your business strategy. Stay aligned with your goals, maintain a strategic approach, and avoid distractions that may jeopardize your success.

The Magick of the Two of Wands Harness the magick of this card and create a vision board. Gather images and symbols that represent your goals and aspirations. Arrange them on the board, infusing each with intentions, and visualize your future success. Display your vision board in a prominent place as a daily reminder.

Words of Wisdom from the Two of Wands When you have balance in your life, there is no struggle.

Spirit Guide—Mouse The Mouse scurries into your life with a warning: focus on the big picture, while tending to the small details. Build a strong foundation but avoid getting bogged down by too many details. Keep moving forward to avoid becoming prey, and keep striving to actualize your vision.

As people are walking all the time,
in the same spot, a path appears.
John Locke

Three of Wands

*Looking into the distance,
at the journey laid out before me
Endless expanse of water, and waves
as far as the eye can see
The full moon shining brightly,
in the midst a sailing ship
Revealing a different way to travel
and continue on my trip*

KEYWORDS & CONCEPTS

LIGHT: group activities, visionary, collaboration, teamwork, overseas ventures, papers and documents, exploration, mutual benefit, travels and journeys, partnerships, executing a plan, preparation, ship's come in, expansion, opportunities, future prospect

SHADOW: narrow view, missed the boat, delayed unions, overlooking details, uncooperative, unrealistic expectations, delaying launch, travel delays or trip postponed, inaction, going nowhere

Scene The Camel longingly looks into the distance, envisioning the endless possibilities laid out before him. Taking a deep breath, he wistfully daydreams, sighing the words "One day." The moon hangs full, illuminating the night's sky. Her light merges with the glow emanating from the tips of the Three Wands, creating a spotlight around the Camel. Feeling the excitement gathering in the night air, he stands in a moment of silence, contemplating the journey ahead, before intentionally moving forward and immersing his front legs into the tepid waters.

The Camel's been preparing for this day a very long time; all packed and getting a feel for the water, he's ready to go. The luminosity of the moon uncovers many modes of transportation available for his journey, either by sky, land, or air. He takes it all in, looking at the panoramic vista before him. The Camel looks down at his legs before glancing up at the balloon, and then across to the sea and outward toward the horizon, resolved to reach his destination by any means possible. Caught in the moment, he blurts out, "Nothing will stand in my way!" Patiently waiting for the right moment, he finds himself slipping into a dreamy world filled with mystery and magick, a place where nothing is, or was, or ever will be; a place of nowhere but everywhere, hidden cleverly in between realms. Shivers run up and down his spine as he falls back into reality. Unperturbed, he confidently continues to stand there waiting for either vessel to reach first, for he's not attached to only one mode of transportation, knowing that as long as he keeps moving forward, he will be successful. Smiling to himself, he whispers softly to the moon, "Everything is going according to plan," just as a thick fog rolls in and blocks his view.

Three of Wands in Love Reminds you that love can thrive in different ways. A partnership built on friendship, transparency, communication, and shared goals can at times surpass traditional notions of romantic love. Embrace love in all its forms and build connections transcending social norms.

Three of Wands in Career Indicates a time of expansion and growth in your business. Welcome new opportunities and take strategic risks. Trust in your creativity; when coupled with intentional planning and a long-term vision, success is on your doorstep.

Three of Wands in Wellness Invites you to embark on a journey, be it a vacation or a retreat. Traveling nurtures the soul and brings a sense of renewal. Take time for you and explore new experiences that uplift the spirit.

Three of Wands in Finances Joint ventures and collaborations hold potential for scaling a business and lucrative rewards. Prior to committing, prioritize a thorough understanding of expectations and your role and scrutinize contracts before implementing. In reference to money, a favorable card, since it talks of expansion and growth.

The Magick of the Three of Wands Dreamscapes into far-off lands, as nodes of moonbeams lull you softly to sleep, facilitating the perfect environment for astral travel, just one of the charms of the Three of Wands.

Words of Wisdom from the Three of Wands Release the tether of the past, embracing new territories and secure opportunities. Let go of old energy patterns to boldly create a future of boundless potential and freedom.

Spirit Guide—Camel The Camel waltzes into your life, bringing the gift of enduring strength and resilience, empowering you to explore new horizons and trust your inner resources. It encourages unwavering determination and the ability to adapt and find nourishment in the most unexpected of places, ensuring success in all endeavors.

I have seen further than others; it is by standing upon the shoulders of giants.
Isaac Newton

Four of Wands

*I stand under the arches of
the home we built
Protecting you always,
with hand upon my hilt
We built a strong foundation,
in perfect harmony
Success is ours, as long as you
stand beside me*

KEYWORDS & CONCEPTS

LIGHT: celebration, stability, cohabitation, achievement, stable plan, milestone, joy, solidarity, domestic life, solid ground, established ideas, security, four corners, the home, fortification, festivals, comforts of home, support

SHADOW: instability, disharmony, unresolved conflicts, cold feet, insecurity, commitment issues, tension, incomplete projects, cohabitating woes, strained relationship, quiet celebration, disconnected, on shaky ground, flimsy ideas

Scene The Peacocks stand under a grand structure, celebrating their accomplishments, gazing deeply into each other's eyes and finding comfort there. This bond comes from years of forging a strong and genuine relationship. The happy couple reflects back on all the planning, all the hard work it took to erect a stable foundation and build a solid life.

    The male Peacock fans out his tail with pride, recapturing her attention, as she flushes sweetly, smiling back. He promised her the world, laid roses

at her feet, took care of her, always making her feel safe and loved. He tilts his chin upward, looking at the sky, grateful that the fates have smiled kindly upon him, for now he gets to call this lovely lady his forever. The female Peacock turns to face her love and says in the sweetest musical voice, "I am so grateful for all your love, your strength, how you hold me in your heart. You are the first thing I see in the morning, and your kiss is the last thing I feel before the night comes to take me away." The male ruffles his feathers and asks, his voice quivering with vulnerability, "I hope you enjoy this home I've built. I've made sure that it'll be comfortable for us and our future." The female Peacock's cheeks fill with a rosy hue as she thinks about the immediate future, absentmindedly patting her belly. He sweeps her up into his arms, waltzing her around the parameter of the Four of Wands, twirling and spreading love and joy into every corner of their humble abode.

Four of Wands in Love Signifies a harmonious and joyful relationship. It represents a time of celebration, stability, and commitment. Whether you are in a partnership or seeking love, this card indicates a positive and fulfilling romantic connection.

Four of Wands in Career This card brings success and stability. Your hard work has paid off with recognition and advancement. Embrace the positive energy and celebrate your achievements, as new opportunities await.

Four of Wands in Wellness Bringing a period of stability, it would indicate "no change" or "stable." If you're inquiring specifically about mental health, improvements are on the horizon as you continue to celebrate small milestones.

Four of Wands in Finances Celebrate your accomplishments and enjoy the rewards of your hard work. It's a positive omen, bringing stability and security especially if you've been facing financial challenges. This card can also signify a new home or property.

The Magick of the Four of Wands Create a gratitude jar. Each day, write down something you're grateful for on a small piece of paper and place it in the jar. Whenever you need a boost of positivity, revisit the jar and read the notes to remind yourself of the abundance in your life.

Words of Wisdom from the Four of Wands The thing is, when you finally choose to build a stable life, it's going to come with a lot of goodbyes.

Spirit Guide—Peacock The Peacock proudly displays its iridescent feathers, reminding you of your own unique beauty and self-expression. Don't play small for anyone; be authentic in all your endeavors by possessing the confidence to proudly showcase your true colors in all your glory. Strut your stuff, let your freak flag fly, and let your freedom inspire others to do the same.

Home is a name, a word, it is a strong one;
stronger than magician ever spoke, or spirit ever answered to,
in the strongest conjuration.
Charles Dickens

Five of Wands

*I am prepared to battle unto
to my death
And will fight until my
last dying breath
I have the strength, with
nothing to fear
To defend the ones I love
and hold dear*

KEYWORDS & CONCEPTS

LIGHT: a cause, competition, disagreements, defending a point of view, squabbles, challenges, raised voices, excitement, conflicting ideas, hassles, fighting for a cause, bickering, friction, rivalry, disturbances, sparring, action required

SHADOW: arguments, fights, overthrow, opposition, challenging someone's ideas, shouting, power struggles, snafu, altercations, ego clashes, feuding, drag-down brawl, offensive positioning, strife, out of control, heated debates, discord, crossed the line, dissonant, no common ground

Scene Colorful Serpents constricting and turning, twisted around the Five of Wands, hissing their disdain with jowls unhinged, ready to strike. They cannot seem to come to a peaceful resolution to their conflicting opinions, so they continue creating strife among themselves, venomously defending their point of view. The red Serpent is exceptionally upset; his rage is palatable, contributing to the energetic chaos of the melee. They all are trying to reason with the blue Serpent, for they need a cohesive unit to complete the mission.

The blue Serpent is totally uninterested in playing nice, since he looks away spitefully from the angry expressions of the rest. The gray Serpent has had enough and is ready to strike; his impatience has gotten the best of him. Done with the blue Serpent's games, the gray Serpent hisses, "This ends now!" Doing her best to reason with the wayward opponent, the pink Serpent tries to deescalate the situation. Doing her best to distract him, she bats her eyelashes, saying, "Hey, big blue." But through the commotion, she's either not heard or completely ignored.

The hissing and shouting escalate as the fiery Wands blaze even brighter, bearing witness to all the discord. The purple Serpent bares his teeth, drawing a breath, and releases it, quickly muttering a curse upon the exhale. The bickering continues with no end in sight. Everyone is holding their position; not one Serpent is willing to bend, for that will show weakness, and here weakness equates to death. The Serpents continue fiercely locking horns, immersed in the clutches of violence, stuck in this endless pattern and completely out of control.

Five of Wands in Love Frequent disagreements can lead to nasty fights in relationships. Prioritize resolving issues swiftly to avoid inner conflict. If single, avoid getting into a competitive mindset when dating, and refrain from pointing out differences to argue about. Drop the combative attitude and heal; this behavior comes from a place of deep pain.

Five of Wands in Career A team effort means not one voice or idea should overshadow another's in group work. Watch out for unhealthful competition and power struggles in the workplace, for it's sure to cause discord among coworkers.

Five of Wands in Wellness Too many ideas create a busy mind, heightening stress levels. Organize your thoughts through writing. Prioritize tasks and then break them down into palatable bites. Balancing stress and conflict is essential for well-being.

Five of Wands in Finances Convoluted and complex financial situations rear their ugly heads. Squabbles regarding finances are very indicative when the Five of Wands is present.

The Magick of the Five of Wands Amid the chaos, conflict reaches its crescendo, signaling imminent resolution. Adopt a calm demeanor by lighting a red candle and saying, "I release strife and embrace inner peace." Blow out the flame and watch conflicts fade away with the wisps of smoke.

Words of Wisdom from the Five of Wands Fighting will get you nowhere, so stop fighting! Here is a stark reminder: you will be leaving this earth with what you came with . . . nothing. So what are you fighting for? Let it go!

Spirit Guide—Serpent When a Serpent slithers into your reading, it carries a big stick! Pay close attention in your dealings with others. The Serpent brings the gift of keen perception, enabling you to decipher vibrational energy, revealing the true intention behind spoken words. Regardless of the severity of any situation, the Serpent empowers you to shed your old skin and embrace growth. It grants you the courage to break free from labels and definitions imposed by others, allowing your authentic self to flourish.

I'm a fighter; I will keep fighting and will never give up.
Marcus Smart

Six of Wands

Hail great victor,
shinning bright as the sun
Fighting for our freedom,
a hero you've become
Highest honor bestowed,
esteemed held so high
Patriot for love of country,
always prepared to die

KEYWORDS & CONCEPTS

LIGHT: victorious, kudos, recognition, acknowledgment, accolades, distinction, awards, praise, spring returns, applause, laurels, honor, conquest, respect, triumphant, homecoming, hero, successful mission, pomp and ceremony, advancement, thumbs up

SHADOW: pride, dishonor, egoism, infamy, recognized for the wrong reasons, humiliation, getting booed, withholding ideas, jealousy, pride, disapproval, criticized, knocked off your high horse, thumbs down, hero complex, negative attention

Scene Waves of adrenaline ripple through the crowd, and deafening cheers rise up, meeting the hero's triumphant return from a successful mission. Crowned the victor, the Tabby Cat enters beneath the canopy of two sturdy trees, passing through the corridor of the Six of Wands. Preening and purring with pride, the hero proudly displays a shiny gold medal adorning his neck, surrounded by swirling orbs, celebrating his remarkable achievements. The

Tabby Cat is seated regally upon his chosen steed, who exemplifies the wisdom of slow and steady, proving that victory belongs to those that persevere. His gaze scans the crowd, seeing their faces. He is a seasoned warrior in the art of war who owes his success to his unwavering vigilance.

The applause crescendos as the hero draws nearer, only to fall eerily silent when he stops and raises his hand to address the crowd. The Tabby Cat narrows his yellow eyes, peering deeply into the gathering as if searching for someone, amid the crowd. Finally zeroing in on one specific face, he clears his throat and says, "I have traveled from afar, and I am deeply grateful for the privilege to address each and every one of you. First, I could have never done this alone, so I take this opportunity to acknowledge the sacrifice of all my fallen comrades, who died a very noble death. I am happy to inform you of our victory today, but it never guarantees the freedom of our tomorrows. Remember what this day feels like. Deeply hold on to it in your heart and never let go, because once it is gone, you'll never get it back. So fight with your last breath, fight for what is just, and, most importantly, fight for your right to be free!" Another thunderous roar of applause ripples through the throng, with people smiling and chanting, "*FREEDOM, FREEDOM, FREEDOM!*" They wave their wands high in the air, showing appreciation for their hero and love of country.

Six of Wands in Love Signifies celebration and victories. Love thrives, bringing admiration and appreciation. Resolve conflicts with respect and communication. If separated, there's a chance of reconciliation.

Six of Wands in Career In the workplace you will be recognized for your achievements. Your hard work and talents are acknowledged, leading to advancements and success. If looking for employment, you will be the victor and awarded with the position.

Six of Wands in Wellness This is a favorable card to see, signifying a period of improved health. Celebrate your progress and continue on the victorious path, overcoming ailments.

Six of Wands in Finances Indicates a successful and prosperous period, especially when asking about business or finances. Everything is lining up and will be met with recognition and success.

The Magick of the Six of Wands This card brings good tidings, sprinkling success on whatever it touches. If you need a bit of extra magick for a victorious outcome, stare into the eyes of the Tabby Cat and request victory.

Words of Wisdom from the Six of Wands Remember that one person's hero is always another's villain.

Spirit Guide—Tabby Cat The Tabby Cat comes purring into your life, bringing the gifts of confidence, independence, and resilience. With its mysterious intrigue, it teaches us to embrace our uniqueness and navigate challenges with grace. This sacred guide brings love, protection, and grounding, reminding you to celebrate victories, stay curious, and always land on your feet.

I believe there is an inner power
that makes winners or losers. And the winners are the ones
who really listen to the truth of their hearts.
Sylvester Stallone

Seven of Wands

*Excitement swirls around me;
I cannot wait for my life to start
An idea burning brightly, tucked away
in the recess of my heart
When I have something precious,
I seem to hold on a bit too tight
My passion is often misunderstood,
but I always do what is right*

KEYWORDS & CONCEPTS

LIGHT: choosing a side, standing up for yourself, defending principles, trying, opposition, resistance, competition, assertiveness, independence, deflection, taking a stand, inner fire, courage

SHADOW: overwhelmed, outnumbered, ego battles, reacting to criticism, defiance, losing ground, unsure of your position, confrontation, noncompliant, being challenged by others, defensive

Scene On a cool evening in the enchanted woods, a Golden Dragon stretches out his glorious wings, protecting the heavy green door that leads into spirit world, where the secrets of the arcana are kept. He holds a blazing wand across his muscular body, daring any one of the other Seven of Wands to try him, for tonight he's not playing. The profuse sweet smell of the black-magic roses hangs heavily in the air, adding to the mystique of the night. He's worked too hard to get to where he is, vowing a long time ago that no one will ever take anything away from him ever again or jeopardize his position, and *this* he's willing to defend to death.

His long tongue whips out and licks the air, tasting fear mingled with the weakness of his opponents. He savors the flavor, rolling it around on his tongue while he levels his gaze. He takes a wide stance, and his heartbeat quickens as the blood rushes to his ears. He revels in taunting his opponents further with his eyes, as a cruel smirk curls on his lips when they cower beneath his scrutiny, making their lighted wands quake and quiver in the darkness. The Golden Dragon takes a purposeful stride toward his targets, fills his chest full of fiery breath, and lets out a blast of fire, giving them a taste of the fury that can be unleashed at a moment's notice if he's pushed any further. The final curls of smoke escape from his nostrils as he opens his mouth and says, "I am the guardian of the realm; I stand on the edge of the world, guarding this portal from anyone or anything that dares to cross before called. Be warned that I will defend my position to death." The opponents' wands dim and waver until completely flickering out, as they quietly slip away into the darkness to regroup and challenge again another day.

Seven of Wands in Love Defensiveness arises from unresolved pain, leading to aggressive communication. Feeling unheard and unseen, as both partners vie for importance. Beware of constant blame shifting, constantly deflecting, and dumping their crap on you, such as "It's always your fault." Address the roots of defensiveness and foster open dialogue.

Seven of Wands in Career In the workplace, you find yourself constantly defending your position. Others may challenge your ideas or seek to undermine your progress. Stand your ground with confidence and showcase your expertise without having to look externally for approval. If you're applying to a new position, this card is indicative of stiff competition.

Seven of Wands in Wellness This card is all about resistance. It can be resistance in seeking medical advice or help, or resistance to medical treatments or medications. The Seven of Wands also highlights defending the right to body autonomy, defending your right to choose what is best for you.

Seven of Wands in Finances In business, this card brings stiff competition and challenges ahead. In the workplace, be assertive when getting your ideas across. Persistence pays off by staying vigilant on the road to success.

The Magick of the Seven of Wands This card gives you the power to confidently voice your opinion. The magick lies in coming up with brilliant ideas that will have to be defended because they will sound too outlandish at first. Keep steadfast in holding on to what you believe, and keep moving forward, pursuing your dream. Light a red candle and say, "I am a force to be reckoned with! I boldly protect my boundaries and use my voice to conquer all obstacles in my path."

Words of Wisdom from the Seven of Wands Some things are worth defending to death. But the wisdom lies in knowing when to let go of something that's already dead.

Spirit Guide—Golden Dragon A rare and discerning spirit guide, the Golden Dragon is very selective of whom it chooses to guide. He is charged with a divine mission to stoke the flames of passion within your soul. This ancient shape-shifter exerts guardianship over all realms, planes of existence, elements, and mysterious forces. Consider yourself blessed to be in the presence of this magnificent golden beast.

A dragon's heart burns fiercely, even in the face of evil.
S. G. Rogers

Eight of Wands

*Against all the odds, I will take
my shot in the dark
Pulling back the bow, willing my
arrow to hit the mark
My desire sends vibrations
through the string of my bow
Success is mine, as long as
I remember to go with the flow*

KEYWORDS & CONCEPTS

LIGHT: penetration, fast progress, multiplying, results incoming, increasing, coming into fruition, hit the ground running, directing energy, quick communication, grounding, taking root, in motion, timing it right, rapid development, materializing, swift action, fast, hitting the mark, excitement, traveling, energetic, keep going

SHADOW: ungrounded, haste, aimless, stunted, inactivity, going against the grain, misguided, missed the mark, falling, withdrawal, running aground, timing's off, apathetic, miscommunication

Scene Under a full moon, the Cheetah races the Eight of Wands by timing it just right and trying to get there before the wands take root. Dragonflies dance in the glen, distracting the Cheetah in order to give the wands a chance to hit their mark and explode into fruition. Excitement pulsates throughout the atmosphere, making the stars shimmer, bearing witness to this glorious occasion by twinkling even brighter in the night sky. Inspired by all the

movement around her, the Cheetah challenges herself even further by testing her speed and prowess against the flight of the wands.

The night surges with magick as golden spirit orbs come by to see what all the commotion is about. Things are moving so fast that time stands still. The Cheetah looks up inquiringly at the wands, daring them to go faster, enjoying this game of speed. Sleek and surefooted, for she was born to run, wild and free, but once the Cheetah sets her sights on something she deeply desires, be sure that she too will always hit her mark. Running even faster, she feels the wind whipping her face, and hears it roaring through her ears. Suddenly she stops; her attention snaps to the left, where she hears a voice coming out of the darkness. Looking up, her nose wrinkles, straining to see if she can catch a scent of the voice's source, but nothing comes. Her ears perk forward as she hears words floating through the air: "You will never 'catch' what you want; the more you chase something, the more it will elude you. Instead, change your frequency, so you can 'attract' what you desire instead of chasing what you want." The Cheetah shakes her head, not even caring about the Eight of Wands game anymore, for this new information really made her think: Why chase something when you can attract something to you? Her lips curl into a smile of satisfaction, as she promptly turns around and casually saunters away.

Eight of Wands in Love Brace yourself for a whirlwind of passion and excitement, for the Eight of Wands is the sex card symbolic of physical penetration. It highlights compatibility, as it fuels the intense sexual chemistry between partners. Get ready to ignite the flames of desire and experience a swift and deep romantic connection. Love is about to get hot and heavy! Also representative of falling in love too quickly, the Eight of Wands could also be indicative of a "quickie."

Eight of Wands in Career Buck up for a thrilling ride in your career. Get ready to experience rapid activity and significant progress. Exciting opportunities will come your way, demanding your attention. A can-do, "YES!" attitude will supercharge your goals into quickly coming to fruition.

Eight of Wands in Wellness When we're ungrounded, everything feels off, and it can lead to increased anxiety and nervousness. To quickly ground yourself, take three deep centering breaths (in through the nose and out through the mouth) and smile.

Eight of Wands in Finances Things are already in motion. Allow abundance to flow effortlessly into your life. A seed was planted long ago, and now the time has come for action. Let your ideas fly, so that they can take root and flourish into abundance. The Eight of Wands also brings swift movement and progress in all financial matters. Opportunities will suddenly arise, demanding quick decisions and action. Keep your eyes open and make the most of the earning possibilities coming your way.

The Magick of the Eight of Wands Ah, the magic of the Eight of Wands calls for a ritual to release all that no longer serves you. Find a secluded spot and unleash a primal yell, letting go of all that pent-up energy. Feel the power as you ground yourself and welcome a renewed sense of balance and vitality. Let it all out and make room for greatness!

Words of Wisdom from the Eight of Wands Let it all go, because you cannot build a life based only on potential.

Spirit Guide—Cheetah Behold the swift Cheetah, a guide of unparalleled speed and tenacity. It ignites your fire by urging you to fearlessly chase your dreams, taking decisive actions to bring them into fruition. Remember, manifestation is a two-way street. Align your intentions and ambition and let the Cheetah guide you to your heart's desires.

When something really really really matters to you,
let it go! Say to the universe: "You know what I want. Give it to me in the
path of least resistance. Give it to me in any way I can get it."
Abraham Hicks

Nine of Wands

In defiance the line is drawn,
standing on guard for thee
Safeguarding all of humanity,
and their right to be free
Hold on to morality, 'cause we're
so running out of time
Believe in the cause and keep shouting
"Hold the line"

KEYWORDS & CONCEPTS

LIGHT: boundaries, guarding, protecting, safeguarding your position, hold your position, tenacity, lone survivor, character, creating personal space, stamina, taking a solid stance, hold the line

SHADOW: putting walls up, defensive, wary, reliving past trauma, battle worn, exposed, overprotective, walls are closing in, overly suspicious, biding time

Scene The Giraffe has traveled from afar, covering much distance well into the night, just for a chance to have an audience with the Fairy Queen. Right at the stroke of midnight, she arrives at the fairy circle. She firmly plants her wands she brought along to create a protective boundary, as she awaits her grace. Surprisingly, the Giraffe spies a luminous transparent butterfly fluttering right above her head. She stares right through it, wondering how it's not getting singed from the torch, making her question if the butterfly was really there at all. A rustling sound is heard coming from the red mushroom, and the Fairy Queen appears in all her glory. Immediately the Giraffe gracefully

bows her long neck, paying homage to the Queen. The Queen's beautiful face contorts, as her ice-blue eyes slowly narrow. She points a bejeweled finger at the Nine of Wands standing sentinel, creating a wall of protection. The Giraffe tilts her head, following the Queen's finger. Puzzled by the Queen's displeasure, she stammers out, "I brought my wands with me, ummm, oh I . . . ahhh . . . it makes me feel better . . ." Her words slowly trail off as the Queen's pointed finger morphs into a palm, stopping the Giraffe's words in midair.

The Queen's musical voice pierces the awkward moment, bringing an eerie chill into the night. She says, "Then the question becomes, Giraffe, is this boundary you erected here to keep others out? Or to keep away the parts of you from causing more pain?" The Giraffe looks stunned as the Queen's words penetrate deep within her soul; she profoundly felt them. Desperately trying to formulate a response, she unsuccessfully bows her head once again, but this time in shame. The Queen's face softens, as a knowing smile slowly reaches her eyes: "Don't fret, tall one. I do understand. Look to the daisies beneath your feet, knowing you will always find a way to survive." As soon as the Queen's words were spoken, a feeling of empowerment hits the Giraffe, emboldening her to straighten out. She stretches up, reaching her full height, and replies in a sure voice, "Thank you."

Nine of Wands in Love Love can be a battlefield, and the Nine of Wands reminds you to stay strong and resilient. Despite past hurts, you have the power to protect your heart while keeping it open. Boundaries are healthful in any relationship, but at times those same boundaries can turn into impenetrable prisons of the past when old wounds are left untended. If single, don't lead yourself on and break your own heart. Be cautious and stick to your dating "deal-breakers."

Nine of Wands in Career Rise above the doubts and express your ideas peppered with passion. Express yourself by using concise communication as you navigate challenges ahead. Your work speaks for itself, so believe in your abilities and let your results do the talking.

Nine of Wands in Wellness Establishing healthful boundaries is a nonnegotiable aspect of happiness. By defining your limits and protecting your energy, you can effectively manage stress. Be mindful of how stress is stored in the body, and incorporate creative ways to release tension. Remember, prioritize the powerful act of self-love.

Nine of Wands in Finances Be brave, hold your position, and prepare for unexpected challenges. Break any barrier to protect your resources, and do whatever it takes to see it through to the end.

The Magick of the Nine of Wands Stop! Just stop keeping others at arm's length for fear of letting them get too close. Stop trying to impress them, for they don't see you. Stop trying to explain yourself, for they don't hear you. You win by fortifying the inside, so anything from the outside, no matter how close the relationship, can never disrupt your inner peace.

Words of Wisdom from the Nine of Wands Beware of defending what no longer deserves your energy. Release attachments to what no longer serves you. Letting go may be difficult, but trying to hold on to something that does not want to stay is even harder.

Spirit Guide—Giraffe The Giraffe brings the gift of rising above. This unique animal is all about having a clear vision and being adaptable. Stretching its graceful neck enables the Giraffe to see things from a different perspective. The Giraffe acts as a bridge between the animals from the world below and the ones belonging to the upper world. Given this unique position, the Giraffe reigns supreme, always able to see the big picture and beyond any boundaries. So stand tall like a Giraffe and conquer the world!

I started to build a home with all the walls
I was putting up for myself, but when I was finished, I realized
I had built a cage and didn't make a key.
Lidia Longorio

Ten of Wands

With every step I struggle,
it's a very hard lesson learned
Pressure put on my shoulders,
I ended up getting burned
I learned a long time ago, the secret is never to give up
Success is guaranteed if I keep trying, vowing not to stop

KEYWORDS & CONCEPTS

LIGHT: determined, completion, responsibilities, grit, purpose, commitments, not giving up, difficult, laborious, trying hard, striving, duty, final push, against all odds, trust yourself, focus on goals, learning lessons

SHADOW: overburdened, obligations, trying too hard, heavy weight, struggling, uphill battle, baggage, strenuous, can't see the road ahead, unbalanced priorities, challenging, overwhelming responsibilities, giving up

Scene The Bumblebee takes a wee rest on a branch strangled by a thick vine. The Bumblebee knows exactly how this sensation of binding feels, since a similar burden is strapped onto his back. The sprouting tufts of greenery give him hope of survival, encouraging him to continue with the promise of a new life. The Bumblebee ponders the burdens of this world as he slowly battles the hills of life. Despite the weight of the Ten of Wands strapped to his back, he raises his head in dignity. Desire burning in his eyes, he takes flight once again, refocused on achieving his goal. He bravely absorbs the impact as the wind continuously slaps him in the face, pushing him backward and preventing him from reaching his destination. Secretly he bears his teeth and struggles with all his might to circumvent the obstacles that lie before him. All semblance of control slips away as he whispers words of encouragement to himself under his labored breaths: "Keep flying, just a little bit more, you're almost there, don't get distracted by minor inconveniences."

A sheen of sweat breaks out across his brow and drips into his eyes, disturbing the line of sight and momentarily causing panic, for he cannot make out the flight path ahead. His body bows as the burden intensifies, weighing him down even more. Suddenly, just when the Bumblebee was about to resign to another pause, golden orbs appear in the night's sky, lighting up a runway ahead. This was the last thing the Bumblebee expected as he mustered the last bit of energy and is guided home.

Ten of Wands in Love The burden of responsibility weighs heavily on the relationship. Time to sit down, talk it out, and find ways to share the emotional load more evenly. You need a partner in love. Settle for nothing less.

Ten of Wands in Career Whoa! Too many "great ideas" or trying to juggle too many things at once is guaranteed to bring unfavorable results. When you're overwhelmed, stuff starts piling up and it becomes a slippery slope of procrastination. Some people are great multitaskers and thrive in busyness, and others are not. The key to success is knowing which one you are.

Ten of Wands in Wellness It's time to lay down the weight of the world you've been carrying on your back. Remember that what you resist persists. So affirm: "The heavy load of my past has no room in my future." Put it down; it's far too heavy to bear.

Ten of Wands in Finances Holding on to your money too tightly does not attract abundance. Loosen your fist a little, for stinginess gets you the exact opposite of what you desire. If financial burdens are weighing you down, evaluate commitments and seek ways to lighten the load.

The Magick of the Ten of Wands Intentionally pick up this card in your hand and focus your attention on the scene. Then think on the burdens you carry and infuse them into the card. Affirm as you lay down the card, "I lay down the weight and set my spirit free. I release the burdens and embrace what will be."

Words of Wisdom from the Ten of Wands Stress arises not from the abundance of tasks, but from their lack of meaning.

Spirit Guide—Bumblebee The Bumblebee comes buzzing with industrious energy, bringing the gift of harmony in your pursuits. By embracing the busy hum of life, remember to take breaks and savor the sweet moments. Your persistence will yield bountiful streams of honey if you can just push through the tough times. The Bumblebee knows that success is really measured by the amount of lessons learned.

> *Believe you can and you're halfway there.*
> **Theodore Roosevelt**

Page of Wands

*Untamed and spirited,
a Page of the fire
I dance with inspiration,
embracing desire
With boundless enthusiasm,
I fearlessly roam
Exploring horizons,
seeking treasures unknown*

KEYWORDS & CONCEPTS

LIGHT: respected, chivalrous, obsessed with an idea, assertive, admirable, outgoing, self-importance, headstrong, hypersexual, antsy, goal oriented, organized, willful, resolve, valiant, adaptive, self-assured, daring, easygoing, born leader, warrior attitude, exuberant

SHADOW: rage, patience worn thin, fiery temper, hypocritical, agitated, seeks vindication, aggressive, reckless, competitive, self-serving, bad temper, irritable, won't ask for help, taking others for granted, self-conscious, needs validation, rebellious

Scene Roaring up to the heavens and shaking his head to and fro, the white tiger unleashes his frustration, which is now teetering on the brink of fury. Tonight everything was going according to plan: he finally managed to get his paws on a flying board. Just the other day, a group of kids came rolling on by, laughing and twisting through the air. He recalls the way he crept in for a closer look at this magickal board. It was his very presence that startled the little group as they fled in a panic, leaving a board behind.

Tonight was supposed to be the night he would finally be free, so tired of all the rules, the pomp and fuss that comes with the title of the Page of Wands. He's so ready to break free and explore unknown horizons, one day to return and become a leader in his own right. He pawed the board, willing it to fly, mimicking what he saw the two-legs do before, but to no avail, not even a budge. The White Tiger looks down to see if he's missing something, and right underneath the board he spies his family's crest on a discarded wooden shield. It was at that moment a golden dragonfly appeared, bringing the words of his father, the King, embossed on her wings:

Son, the day will come when you will sit on my throne
You're the one who's next in line, for you're my firstborn
Enjoy this time now, for you will never be as young or free
Son, when you're doubting life, promise you'll remember me

With that, the White Tiger dismounts the board and forcefully shoves it out of the way with his nose. He gingerly picks up the forgotten shield and straps it onto his back. Then he turns around and saunters through the front door, announcing, "Hey, everybody, I'm home!" He mischievously smiles and mutters under his breath, "For now."

Page of Wands in Love Commitment is difficult for this Page because he requires a lot of freedom and blind trust from a partner. He enjoys spending time together but requires an equal amount of time alone. He cherishes his independence and needs a partner who can match his energy on adventures. The Page of Wands shows his love through physical affection, demanding emotional intimacy, so he can let his guard down and feel safe. He requires respect and appreciation. If not, he will stray and satisfy his "freak in the sheets" tendencies elsewhere.

Page of Wands in Career Loyal and devoted to his job, this Page craves new experiences in order to keep boredom at bay. Love for his independence makes this Page a great entrepreneur, or digital nomad, since he always finds himself gravitating toward odd careers to quell his wanderlust. Although he never stays long, because he abhors being pigeonholed into one role. This Page would be well suited working in the travel industry.

Page of Wands in Wellness Headaches, running hot, high blood pressure, fevers, hot flashes, overheating... most of these issues are created from being constantly overstressed. Watch out for head injuries and concussions, for they are common for this Page.

Page of Wands in Finances This Page makes a good investor because by nature they're not overly emotional. They do very well playing the stock market, because cool heads prevail, despite their hearts racing with excitement and passion, a true enigma.

The Astrological Sign of the Page of Wands Aries (March 21–April 19)

Words of Wisdom from the Page of Wands Celebrate your fiery essence. Let it blaze through your every step and illuminate the world with the brilliance of your soul.

Spirit Guide—White Tiger A sacred animal of royalty, the White Tiger comes purring into your life to let you know how special you truly are. The pure heart of this rare mystical beast beats with love for all living things. When channeling the energy of the White Tiger, welcome it into your life as your muse. It will reward you with passion and ignite the ember of creativity, stoking the fires within.

Arian anger flashes forth with the speed of sound,
but it's usually gone before the victim knows what it's all about,
and the happy, childlike smile quickly returns.
Linda Goodman

Knight of Wands

*A hazard to myself,
please set me free
Sometimes I'm my own
cruelest enemy
The passion that bubbles
burns so hot
If ever in trouble, I break out
into a trot*

KEYWORDS & CONCEPTS

LIGHT: bringer of messages, communicates through words, ruled by ideas, adventurous, potential suitor, flamboyant, steadily moving forward, dynamic, idolizing something or someone, warrior energy, banter, risk taker, excitable, tease, boisterous, instinctual

SHADOW: mouthy, hotheaded, protective of his energy, hyper, wild, taunting, overtly sexual, easily bored, sweet talker, rebel, lacking control, intolerance, mishandling situations, lacking emotional maturity, trouble settling down, inconsistent

Scene Sprinting through the King's Woods, the Knight of Wands casts a warm glow into the darkness of midnight, alighting the whole area with the fiery energy coursing through his veins. Priding himself on being "the black sheep" of the bunch, he's always dashing off, finding himself somewhere between lost and found. Clipping along with a lively canter, he suddenly stops, finding the perfect spot where he can see *Her*, the moon, shining full of glory. His hooves are firmly planted within the sacred grove, feeling the

energy pulse up from Mother Earth's core. He leans his head back, enthralled in ecstasy, his pulse visibly pounding in his thick corded neck, joining Gaia in the eternal fiery dance. Neighing in frustration, he exhales the excess warrior energy, the tendrils of fire escaping his nostrils leaving wisps of smoke in their wake. As if answering his call, a gust of wind taunts him, joining in on the wild dance, tossing his mane mercilessly into the wind.

Tonight he's wound way too tight as he vigorously shakes his head, trying to dispel the thoughts quickly flooding his mind. How ironic that the master of words could also be at the very mercy of those same words if arranged in a different order. Thoughts quickly bubble to the surface of how all those times in the throes of passion, that fiery devilish tongue got him into trouble. It was in this very moment the Knight of Wands decided that he's done; this is where he leaves it, right here on this hallowed ground. He stretches up to touch the stars, pawing at the sky, with powerful hind legs supporting his decision to let go of it all. A long shrill echoes throughout the woods as he unleashes all his fury, landing back down with a thunderous thud cracking the ground. He's free, and he exercises that right as he careens in the opposite direction, dashing off to look for his next conquest.

Knight of Wands in Love The boyfriend card. When asking about love and the Knight of Wands appears, it's a great indication that someone might be entering your life, with potential for a romantic relationship. Caution is necessary, for this Knight does have a roving eye, and when bored he'll look elsewhere for stimulation.

Knight of Wands in Career In any career, the Knight of Wands needs continual stimulation in order to be happy and stay in a position. He's lively and interesting, bringing a lot of energy into any workplace. Everybody knows his name and has a story about this Knight. If you're looking for work, variety should be a featured component to any job description you're interested in, for this Knight will wither in any environment that has repetitive, monotonous tasks.

Knight of Wands in Wellness When the Knight of Wands appears, it's indicative that something is either happening quickly or clearing up quickly.

Look to the surrounding cards for an indication of what direction the Knight is moving and the particulars.

Knight of Wands in Finances Encourages you to take risks when it comes to moneymaking ideas. With any new venture, make sure that all the pros and cons are weighed out prior to taking the leap. The Knight of Wands is very indicative that a side hustle could turn out very profitable.

The Movement of the Knight of Wands The Knight of Wands represents aspects associated with fire signs. As bringers of messages and the embodiment of pure energy, all Knights represent energy and speed of timing. In regard to timing, the Knight of Wands is the second-fastest Knight—he dashes and careens, moving at a very fast and erratic speed. Not as fast as his counterpart the Knight of Swords, but he's right up there and can hold his own. He brings messages of inspiration.

Words of Wisdom from the Knight of Wands You can run, but you will never be able to hide from the hardships and lessons of life, for they will shape you into the person you were meant to be.

Spirit Guide—Black Stallion The Black Stallion is known for its beauty and grace, a true showstopper bred for pleasure and procreation. This stud knows how to attract the ladies, while he himself can be a bit unpredictable; as a self-proclaimed bachelor, it makes it difficult to get him to commit and settle down. Charismatic and charming, he gallops into your life, bringing the gift of passion and reminding you that with everything you do, make sure you feel something; stop going through the motions. Embrace the fiery embers that burn within your soul: express them, embrace them, ignite them. Fan the flames and coax them into a raging inferno. To keep this Knight's attention, he needs constant physical touch and gentle words, just like the Black Stallion, or he will take off to explore something else that grabs his attention.

It may be easy to get on that high horse, but the fall is a bitch.
Aimee Vernon

Queen of Wands

With me, you have one shot,
so tread carefully, my friend
Prove yourself to be worthy,
and my loyalty won't bend
No time to waste on someone who's
not what they seem
I can be your darkest nightmare,
or your sweetest dream

KEYWORDS & CONCEPTS

LIGHT: muse, devoted, generous, integrity, inspiring, creative, eloquent, protective, passionate, proud, confident, center of attention, strong willed, admired, courageous, bewitching, loud, gifted, talkative, extra, bold, touchy, instinctive, affluential, ingenious

SHADOW: overreactive, arrogant, highly opinionated, self-centered, commanding, makes excuses, checks out easily, indifferent, egotistical, condescending, selfish, show-off, insistent, diva, boastful, theatrical, control freak, indignation, attention seeker, on the warpath, fierce, instigator

Scene Liquid pools of burnt amber level their gaze in your direction, as the Queen of Wands' strong energy makes her presence known. Frozen, you dare not look away, for it will show weakness, yet softening your gaze so as not to inadvertently challenge her grace. Rising to occasion, the confidence rolling off her aura is so overwhelming, making your breath hitch, not daring another look. The lioness slowly tilts her head to the side, expectingly waiting for you to speak. You open your mouth, but nothing comes out. There is

nothing you can do to rip your focus away from that crowning vision of perfection before you. Briefly closing your eyes, you resign, allowing your fate to take the reins. The Queen of Wands' eyes glitter with knowing as she begins to loudly purr—the vibrations felt throughout your body is quite shocking—as you snap your mouth shut at a loss for words.

The woods are thrown into an eerie quietness as all activity hangs on the breath and words of this majestic being. "I'm glad you finally came, for I have been waiting. What you feel coursing through your body is the frequency of my healing vibrations, for you are not right and haven't been for a while now." Stunned at the revelation, you hang your head, allowing her words to deeply penetrate into your psyche. A tear rolls down your cheek as you manage to whisper, "How did you know?" The Queen gives you a lazy smile and says, "Ah, little one. I have watched you for a while now, walking to and fro, acting like the world's on fire, always looking for yourself in all the wrong places."

The Queen holds up her perfectly manicured paw, where a tiny flame appears. Amazed, you watch in wonder as the dancing flame is reflected in her eyes. "I have magick dominion over the element of fire. Take this tiny spark, knowing that no matter what happens, you're never alone. This tiny spark will change everything; all you have to do is believe." With that she removes her bracelet, offering you the Amulet of Protection, and then the flame. Looking down at your wrist, you marvel at the fit, admiring its intricate design, the tiny flame now dancing in your palm. Bowing low in gratitude to the Queen, you take your leave, walking away smiling and shaking your head, coming to the conclusion that it's the Queen of Wands' world, and we all just live in it!

Queen of Wands in Love To capture the heart of this fiery Alpha, you have to prove your worth and match her energy without competing with her. The way through to her heart is with admiration, and many compliments. The biggest turnoff for this royal is desperation or weakness in a partner, and her biggest turn-ons are strength, honesty, and loyalty.

Queen of Wands in Career She blazes a trail in the workplace, harnessing her fiery passion and monumental confidence. Embrace your natural leadership, unleash your creativity, and set the world ablaze with your ideas. Inspire others with your magnetic presence and fearlessly pursue your ambitions.

Queen of Wands in Wellness She ignites her wellness with laughter, tossing her glorious and flowing mane as she roars with soulful delight. She hides her vulnerability well, perceiving it as weakness, yet shares emotions secretively. Nurture your heart's fiery beat and maintain circulation's dance to keep the lifeblood flowing throughout your body.

Queen of Wands in Finances She commands her finances with passionate determination, igniting creative opportunities to sow the seeds of abundance. She exudes confidence in her financial ventures, taking calculated risks and seizing the throne of wealth. Her magnetic charisma attracts prosperity and material success. She wisely manages resources, ensuring a stable and prosperous kingdom. Embrace her entrepreneurial spirit and conquer the world.

Astrological Sign of the Queen of Wands Leo (July 23–August 22)

Words of Wisdom from the Queen of Wands Remember, I am not only the Queen, honey. I'm the whole bloody kingdom!

Spirit Guide—Lioness Her Royal Highness struts into your life, bringing gifts of courage, confidence, and protection. Her loyalty is extraordinary, because once she considers you part of her pride, she'll never leave your side. Her confidence is so palatable and her lesson paramount: "As sovereign of your own nation, there is no higher authority than yourself."

I am mine before I am anyone else's.
Nayyirah Waheed

King of Wands

I get bored way too easily;
life's a great adventure full of fun
Honey, if you can't run with
the big boys, you're not the one
By holding on too tightly,
I'll slip through your hands
I'll wander and roam in other places,
exploring uncharted lands

KEYWORDS & CONCEPTS

LIGHT: entrepreneur, optimistic, fun, honest, travel lover, originality, detail oriented, social, aloof, uninhibited, bold, adventurous, thoughtful, free spirit, independent, nice, witty, conversationalist, curious, straightforward, goofy

SHADOW: absentminded, hot tempered, egomaniac, impatient, fears commitment, apprehensive, rude, short tempered, bossy, overly confident, emotionally reserved, overly eager, restlessness

Scene The King of Wands prides himself on being able to do as he pleases, to run free, to explore new areas, and to go on wild adventures. Then, he finds the highest ledge overlooking his kingdom and lies in the sun all afternoon, lost in his daydreams. A smile touches his lips as he says, "It's great to be the King." In his realm, every day is just as pleasurable as the last, until today . . . today he woke up with that familiar pit in his stomach, for today is the day he dreads all year long; today is the absolute worst day! Once a year this whole sordid ordeal hangs over his head, the horrid evening when all his subjects come before him to air their grievances. Reluctantly the King of Wands mounts his dais as growing frustration causes him to rub the back of his neck with extreme agitation. He's been kept waiting for quite a while now and snarls out, "Who dares to keep the King waiting? I'm the king of the jungle, tattooed badass, lover of the ladies, and if ever in doubt, just look. I have a great big crown to prove it!"

He lowers the finger pointing to his head, pissed as he wonders how long this is going to take before he can get back to having fun before sundown. He roars even louder, expressing his extreme displeasure, making the ground quake in fear, just as the velvet curtains start parting as he casually reaches up a claw to straighten his crown. From above he hears the first name announced. Disinterested, the King looks down, focusing on some random orb, wishing he was anywhere but here. He snarls, "State your case." Upon hearing the subject's voice, his angry yellow eyes snap up to meet an old, wrinkly, familiar face. He jumps up; the crown clangs to the ground. He paces quickly back and forth, annoyed and muttering to himself, swishing his tail, swatting at imaginary flies. He can't hold it in anymore, all semblance of control whooshed out as he forcefully addresses his subjects. "Nope, nope, I will not do one more! Tortoise and the Hare, or whatever came first, the Chicken or the Egg—no way, I'm DONE!" And with that, the King turns tail and runs as fast and far as he can, climbing up the first tree he finds, high enough to watch the sun go down.

King of Wands in Love This King is a bold and passionate lover, a ball of sexual energy who needs regular stimulation and excitement in his relationship. He doesn't shy away from his feelings, having no qualms about letting you know exactly how he feels, courtesy of his fiery temper.

King of Wands in Career The King of Wands is highly competitive and views the workplace as a contest of skills, making them great entrepreneurs or business partners. They have an insatiable hunger for acquiring new business, clients, and contracts.

King of Wands in Wellness The king of excess energy, exercise becomes paramount to help regulate this fiery King. A balanced wellness routine will serve this King well and help bring down blood pressure.

King of Wands in Finances As a take-control kinda guy, the King of Wands knows exactly how much money he has. For this King, the amount of money directly correlates with his freedom. And be sure, nothing is getting in the way of his freedom!

The Astrological Sign of the King of Wands Sagittarius (November 22–December 21)

Words of Wisdom from the King of Wands If you are displeased now, in a few years you will be even more displeased, but older. So take action now and change the story.

Spirit Guide—Lion The majestic Lion, king of the jungle, supreme ruler of the realm, has come to awaken your inner power. Reclaim what's rightfully yours and step into your greatness. Be courageous, stand up for your beliefs, and roar your truth for all to hear. Let the Lion guide you to a reign of absolute authenticity and personal best.

I am not afraid of an army of lions led by a sheep;
I am afraid of an army of sheep led by a lion.
Alexander the Great

Ace of Cups

*Within my soul's sacred depths,
emotions ebb and flow
A reflection of love, where my heart
finds solace to grow
Desires bloom like an eternal spring;
a treasure never wanes
Chalice Well's healing embrace,
intuition's elixir sustains*

KEYWORDS & CONCEPTS

LIGHT: immortality, adoration, emotional fulfillment, opportunity in love, in tune, humanity, happy news, emotionally available, idolize, new attitude, water element, acceptance, favor, preliminary stages, desires, enamored, openness, spirit, universal source

SHADOW: living in a fantasy world, hurt by loving someone, selfish, feelings spill out, pining for love, overwhelming emotions, feeling empty, love obsession, messy, needy, unrequited love

Scene A beautiful ornate cup sits in the middle of a languid Pool of Atonement, displaying the highest expression of love. A bouquet of velvety red roses fills the cup, creating a heady scent of perfume that lingers in the air. Watching the joyful dance of the flying fish reminds you of the sadness that brought you here. With a heavy, thoughtful sigh, you deeply inhale the aroma of rose hanging in the air. Immediately your chest starts to feel lighter, as the pain surrounding your heart miraculously loosens up a bit. You notice

a downed log at the edge of the pond, and you take a seat to reflect upon the Ace of Cups shimmering before you.

Being fully present in the here and now, you sit for what seems like forever, not wanting to break the magickal spell of this surreal moment. After a while your thoughts turn to what brought you here: LOVE. Unexpectedly there's a break in the silence as you hear the utterance of a soft song emanating from the Ace of Cups, notes swirling as the melody wraps around you, creating a blanket of peace. Cocking your head to one side, picking up the words drifting toward you from the hallows of the woods, you realize that the trees have joined in harmony. Listening intently, you hear these words:

> *I release you with compassion and love*
> *I release you to fly on the wings of a dove*
> *I release you, because you were never mine*
> *Trust me when I say I'll be just fine*
> *I release you, to make room in my heart*
> *Because the time has come for us to part.*

You feel the throb of your heartbeat hammering in your chest, as the words burrow deeply into your heart. Releasing a breath you were holding, a tear softly slips down from the corner of your eye until it falls into the pool, joining the waters. With reverence, you quietly get up and whisper, "Thank you" to the Ace of Cups and turn away, knowing that today marks a fresh start, and, more importantly, realizing that you too are deserving of a happily ever after.

Ace of Cups in Love Dive into the boundless depths of love's reservoir. Surrender to the currents of love and allow emotions to surge forth and intertwine. Existing relationships thrive through heartfelt vulnerability and honest communication. Immerse yourself in the intoxicating elixir of love's infinite possibilities.

Ace of Cups in Career Signifies a profound shift in your career path. A surge of enthusiasm and creative energy flows, making you crave a deeper connection to your work, a purpose. Embrace new opportunities that resonate with your soul and align with your passions, then watch abundance flow.

Ace of Cups in Wellness The heart's harmony reflects vitality within. Unblock stagnant energy by releasing emotions, allowing a free flow through the chakras. Dissolve emotional and physical barriers, finding healing through authentic expression. Sometimes "a good ol' cry" is all it takes.

Ace of Cups in Finances Financial abundance is attracted when you align your heart's desires with your financial decisions. Intuition becomes a guiding light, leading you to make choices in line with your passions that bring fulfillment. Paying it forward, coupled with a positive mindset, creates a harmonious flow of wealth into your life.

The Magick of the Ace of Cups The Ace of Cups represents the fusion of divine and earthly energies, offering a profound sense of unity. It allows for potent divination practices such as scrying and tasseomancy, fostering deep connections and revealing the oneness of all beings. Embrace this powerful spiritual energy for magickal exploration. <u>Love Tea:</u> Brew a magickal infusion by combining rose petals, lavender, and cinnamon. Let it steep in boiling water, strain, and sip to ignite the flames of love.

Words of Wisdom from the Ace of Cups I am a pool of reflection. Look deeply into my cup and see yourself reflected back with loving eyes.

Spirit Guide—Flying Fish Behold the graceful Flying Fish, a guide bringing the gift of fluidity. It encourages you to navigate and adapt through life's challenges with agility. Dive into new experiences, soar above limitations, and trust your instincts to find the freedom and abundance that awaits.

Love is composed of a single soul inhabiting two bodies.
Aristotle

Two of Cups

*Two hearts entwined in deep waters,
a cosmic dance of love
Souls aligned in enchantment,
as harmony descends from above
Soulmates united throughout the
ages, with a haunting melody
The universe conspired to entwine
us; only love can set us free*

KEYWORDS & CONCEPTS

LIGHT: marriage, a couple, intimacy, romantic relationship, joining, conversations, harmony, equality, engagement, wedding or handfasting, compatibility, mutual attraction, connection, balance, romantic partners, opposites attract, reuniting, karmic ties, new union

SHADOW: disconnect, stringing someone along, wishy-washy, platonic relationship, one-sided love, estrangement, only friends, unbalanced relationship, wavering, distrust, mismatched, abandoned, superficial love, uncommitted

Scene At the edge of a shimmering pond, two lovers share intimate moments amid the enchanted grove, their love sparking off the dripping diamonds adorning the Two of Cups. The sprigs of greenery offer a perfect canopy of privacy over the aquamarine pool as the lovers gaze into each other's eyes, joined in a passionate union. Their palpable connection intensely throbs between the them, causing small ripples in the pond of love. The Seahorses feel whole as the divine masculine energy joins with the divine feminine

energy, uniting them in this erotic dance of give and take: where one lacks, the other fills the void. The arc of water joins the lovers, displaying the climax of a harmonious spiritual union. Even as individuals, their souls will be forever connected throughout the ages, for true love is immortal.

Floating atop the water lilies, the bejeweled Two of Cups grants them qualities needed for a successful union, bestowing them with beauty, trust, communication, equality, and love, all endearing qualities needed in a loving relationship. The lovers stay locked in each other's embrace, tails entwined, and will forever drift toward each other even when they are worlds apart. He looks at her dead in the eye and says, "I am always with you" and seals those words with a passionate kiss, entangling them eternally together.

Two of Cups in Love A sacred union blooms, weaving an important thread in the tapestry, imbued with deep connection and divine romance. It signifies a significant relationship, usually romantic in nature, but can signify any partnership with karmic connections.

Two of Cups in Career Symbolizes the power of partnership and collaboration. By joining forces with another who shares your vision, you can create synergistic opportunities propelling your career to new heights.

Two of Cups in Wellness Dive deep into your emotional connections. Explore the power of intimacy, vulnerability, and shared experiences. Aspire to achieve balance, where everyone's voice is heard equally and differences are celebrated. Engage in heart-centered practices by looking for verbal and nonverbal cues to further your heart connection, especially with things you don't accept or understand.

Two of Cups in Finances This card indicates exploring mutually beneficial opportunities such as pooled investments, mutual funds, and joint accounts, or merging finances, mergers, and business partnerships. Build solid financial relationships to create abundance and increase your wealth together.

The Magick of the Two of Cups Unleash the magick of the Two of Cups, where cosmic equilibrium seeks to dance amid the light and shadow. Immerse yourself in romance, intertwining heart, mind, body, and soul. Let songs of love serenade your heart, and stories of love ignite your passion, and feel the rhythm of the words unfold in waves, harmonizing with your soul's melody.

Words of Wisdom from the Two of Cups Acceptance is the magickal potion in the chalice. Embracing others as they are nurtures authentic connections that resonate with soulful love.

Spirit Guide—Seahorse As a revered creature of Poseidon, the Seahorse brings the gift of eternal love. With sacred intuition, it fosters deep connections and cherishes partnerships. Embracing monogamy and lifelong devotion, it illuminates the path to love, guiding you toward the transformation of the soul's eternal bond.

> *When seahorses find a mate,*
> *they wrap their tails around each other so the tide*
> *doesn't drift them apart. They have one mate for the rest of*
> *their lives. When the mate dies, they do too.*
>
> **Unknown**

Three of Cups

*Dance the spiral dance of creation;
embrace your wild side
Celebrate the soul awakened,
on this wild and crazy ride
Stand tall amid life's tempest; draw
strength from her gale
With an unbridled spirit together,
our magick we'll unveil*

KEYWORDS & CONCEPTS

LIGHT: friendships, companionship, throuple, celebrations, rejoicing, social circle, delight, festivities, dancing, midsummer, polyamory, extrovert, creative collaborations, singing, spark of life, hedonism, not taking love too seriously, threesomes, more the merrier, together, support, gatherings, achievements

SHADOW: getting carried away, not taking life seriously, agoraphobia, partying too much, introverted, fake smile, antisocial, few friends, trying to find a spark, three's a crowd, unfulfilled, noncommittal, FOMO (fear of missing out)

Scene Fathoms deep at the bottom of the sea, the Octopus casts his thoughts of merrymaking into the watery depths, as an invitation for others to come and join the party. He's eager for the festivities to commence. A party hat is placed jauntily atop his head, while a spectacular array of balloons and party favors are on display for his guests. He's a true believer in the concept of the more the merrier, because love is meant to be multiplied. The Octopus knows how special these social occasions are, for it brings people closer together

through shared experiences. A few guests have finally arrived, and not able to contain his joy, the Octopus holds his arms out, wiggling them in a welcoming gesture, as the other arms wildly swing the Three of Cups in excitement. The starfish, hearing the sounds of celebration, gather around to see what all the commotion is about. They too get caught up in the joyous occasion by releasing bubbles of laughter that escape up to the human world, popping with a resounding hiccup and giggle.

Above the watery depths, you are sitting alone on the beach, contemplating the doldrums of life. Overwrought with emotion, you shake your fists to the sky, imploring the universe for a sign. Suddenly you hear a pop and something sounding like laughter. Unsure, your ears perk up as you look around, making sure you're still alone. The coast is clear, only you and your shadow of sadness. Instantaneously it dawns on you—that's your sign! Snorting and grabbing your belly as you double over with uncontrollable laughter, amazed that's all it took: a few bubbles on the surface of the water dripping with irony, as your "sign" laughs at you! You make the connection of the symbolism, and the message of not to take yourself or life too seriously. You marvel at the power of the universe and wonder how much we don't know about the bottomless oceans of human emotions.

Three of Cups in Love Yearning for fulfillment, this card embraces the spirit of throuples and threesomes. Here, everyone's honored and loved equally, seeking to master jealousy and possess the confidence to give yourself fully. Love is meant to be shared freely, since its truest form knows no bounds. This card invites immense joy and brings pleasure into any union.

Three of Cups in Career The Three of Cups sings the praises of teamwork and collaborations. It signifies the magick of getting along with others in the workplace, creating an atmosphere of harmony and shared success. This card represents work gatherings, company parties, and workplace celebrations. When it comes to business, this card is indicative of corporate mergers and conglomerates.

Three of Cups in Wellness Embrace life's richness, finding joy in every moment, and dance with wild abandon. Curate self-love and create a space that fosters genuine happiness to flourish. In matters of health, this card offers potential for healing, during the celebration of life.

Three of Cups in Finances Heralds prosperous collaborations and shared financial goals. Embrace the potent synergy of networking and community support. If seeking financial support, help is on the way. However, be mindful of overspending on recreational pursuits, or too much partying.

The Magick of the Three of Cups Three of Candles Ritual: Light three candles—a green one for gratitude, symbolizing appreciation and growth, a pink one for harmony, invoking love and balanced relationships, and a gold one for abundance, manifesting prosperity and opportunities into your life.

Words of Wisdom from the Three of Cups Drink your fill from the chalice of life. Savor the taste of what it feels to be alive, floating in this infinite moment of time.

Spirit Guide—Octopus The octopus brings the gift of community, emerging from the inky depths to guide you. Embrace its fluid grace and resourcefulness, navigating through problems with ease. Like the octopus, foster genuine connections embracing the magick of community. Unleash your creativity, drawing from diverse talents, and paint your canvas of life. Let the octopus be your guide in weaving symbiotic connections and embrace the magick of shared connections.

*I celebrate the connections in my life, from my past, present, and future.
I joyfully accept love in all its healthy forms!*
Amy Leigh Mercree

Four of Cups

*Fixated on my empty cups,
where waters no longer flow
Bored and disconnected,
self-loathing pawn refusing
to grow
Fortune smiles upon the lucky;
cups brim with endless cheer
Yet, I swim in the muddy waters
of life, seeking a new frontier*

KEYWORDS & CONCEPTS

LIGHT: yearning for someone, in your feelings, discontentment, boredom, reevaluating your relationship, daydreaming, worrying, guarded, unavailable, unaware, missing piece, tunnel vision, help is on the way!

SHADOW: stunned, unresponsive, speechless, festering, unexpressed emotions, emotionally unavailable, apathy, fixated on someone unavailable, needing space, self-deprecating behavior, pity party, despair, numb, distant, melancholy

Scene The Beta fish is looking for something more. Lately he's become so dissatisfied; it seems as if the world around him is closing in, and feels like it's getting smaller every day. His daily musings lead him to the same conclusion that something is missing. With a forlorn expression, he focuses on the empty cups in his bowl, wondering, "How? How's this possible? To be surrounded by all this water, and my cups still remain empty!" The Beta swims around the edge of consciousness, dejected and brooding, falling into a strange silence. He peers into the distance, slipping mercifully into a daydream.

Teasing him, out of the corner of his eye, he sees the missing green cup, wavering in and out of his vision. His chest tightens as he lets out a frustrated sigh. Tiny little bubbles come out of his mouth and float up to the surface. Until that moment, he didn't even realize he was holding his breath underwater. The irony. Vindicated, he stares at the vision before him, remaining tight-lipped and frozen in place so as not to disrupt the enchantment. This is the missing cup! The last one needed to complete his set; the Four of Cups, zoning into the green cup and contemplating his next move.

You walk into the room, your eye catching on the fish bowl. Scratching your head, you try to remember if you fed the fish today. Oh well. "Here fishy, fishy, fishy, dinner time," you say as you take a generous pinch of fish flakes between your fingers, sprinkling it on the water. "There you go, fish; now it's time for momma to have her treat too." You grab your green wineglass and toast the fish. Taking a sip, you walk out of the room with wineglass in hand.

Four of Cups in Love If boredom is settling into your relationship, it's time to spice things up and switch it up a bit by exploring fantasies and deep desires together. If looking for love, there are many romantic opportunities coming your way, but you are not noticing them.

Four of Cups in Career Become cognizant of opportunities coming up in your career. Soon you will be offered something such as a new responsibility, a title, or a promotion. In order to reap these rewards, first you must focus on seeing the opportunity, then acting on it.

Four of Cups in Wellness Time to get out of your funk! The Four of Cups is here to remind you that you and only you are in control of your own well-being. Stop looking outward for a savior. Be your own superhero and get on with it.

Four of Cups in Finances Don't focus too hard on one financial prospect and miss the forest for the trees. Here is where you have to create an opportunity for yourself, regardless if you see it there or not. Trust that there are many viable ways to create the abundant life you desire, and methodically work toward that vision.

The Magick of the Four of Cups As if by magick, an opportunity will be created out of thin air and will come in the most unexpected way. All you have to do is get out of your own way and recognize the opportunity when it presents itself.

Words of Wisdom from the Four of Cups Ask yourself, would you rather be comfortable or happy? There is a whole world out there waiting for you to explore. No one deserves to stay in an arid space that is starved of joy.

Spirit Guide—Beta Fish The Beta Fish brings the gift of panorama, reminding you that before going on the warpath, look at the situation from all vantage points before making any moves. This brave fish comes swimming into your life to gently awaken the warrior within, letting you know that sometimes the most healthful thing you can do is draw a line in the sand and defend that stance with everything you have. Never fear of fighting alone, since the Beta will always have your back.

We're just two lost souls,
swimming in a fish bowl year after year
Running over the same old ground,
what have we found?
"Wish You Were Here" by Pink Floyd

Five of Cups

*In sorrow's abyss, solace's
whispers fade away
Loss and regret, a haunting
price to pay
From spilled cups, a
bitterness takes hold
Hope succumbs, swallowed
by shadows cold*

KEYWORDS & CONCEPTS

LIGHT: grieving, not seeing eye to eye, not all is lost, learning from your mistakes, rocky relationship, forgiveness, reassessing life, setbacks, emotional upset, glass half full, gloomy, moody, renewed perspective

SHADOW: hurt, despondent, feeling rejected, disappointed, loss, despair, self-pity, remorse, regret, unhappy, dejected, blaming others, relationship obstacles, living in the past, sadness, clumsy, hopeless, devastated, wallowing in misery, glass half empty, failure, imagining the worst

Scene The Penguin hangs her head despondently, chin trembling as she feels the raw hurt coursing through her body, bowing her shoulders from all the weight. A shimmering tear slips out of the corner of her eye as her body wracks with sobs, mourning the loss of something that never came to be. She tries to hide her pain as a vacant expression crosses her face. She still wears the veil, which was once as white as the bouquet of calla lilies she holds, but has now turned black like the ashes left behind in her heart. All

she wants is to be left alone to grieve, not wanting anyone's pity, for she has enough of her own to last a lifetime.

She hopelessly looks down at three cups lying on their sides, kicking one and feeling just as hollow. A part of her hoped they were full so she could drown her sorrows, put out the fires, and quell the acrid bitterness in her throat from too many tears, too many lies, too many times, engulfed by ugly words over the years that couldn't be swallowed. The moonlight catches her attention, and as she turns her head following the illumination, her gaze settles on the middle arch. The night lays its mantle of darkness on her shoulders. Losing track of time, she shivers, reassuring herself, "The nights are always the hardest." She turns her body around to look at the source of light, wishing at this moment that she could erase the moon and plunge the world into total darkness. Lost in thought, her gaze clouds over, mesmerized by the motes of light reflecting off something to the side. Turning to look, she sees two more cups, but these ones are filled to the brim, now bringing the total to the Five of Cups. Apologetically, her rueful eyes rest back on the moon, and she wisely says, "I'm sorry."

Five of Cups in Love Even though you are deep into your feelings, not all is lost. The relationship may be salvaged, for two of the cups still stand. Time to reevaluate and find out where both of you stand, by clarifying your expectations moving forward. If single, don't lose hope; there is somebody for everybody—you are just looking in the wrong places.

Five of Cups in Career Feeling let down at work and unappreciated, finding it difficult to concentrate on the task at hand. Regroup and ask yourself if you can make this work—can you be happy in this environment? If not, it's time to look for something better suited for you. If looking for work, you won't find it where you're looking.

Five of Cups in Wellness Dealing with grief and loss, wondering, "What if I can't let go?" This card brings sorrow and is indicative that there are deep wounds that haven't quite healed. The time has come to mourn the loss of that someone or something. It's true that time heals, but it's also true the soul never forgets. This is also the card of addictions and substance abuse.

Five of Cups in Finances You may be focusing on what you don't have rather than trying to salvage and build on what you do actually have. Remember, when the money is gone, it's gone! The focus of the Five of Cups is to start rebuilding your wealth; not all is lost.

The Magick of the Five of Cups Nudges you to take a good look around. The answers and signs are there, but you just haven't noticed them yet. It's in the moment when all seems lost that the magick of the Five of Cups comes in, offering you a glimmer of hope.

Words of Wisdom from the Five of Cups I will no longer build my home in the hearts of people that didn't mean to say "forever" after the words "love you."

Spirit Guide—Penguin The Penguin, a steadfast spirit guide, waddles into your life, helping you navigate life's ebbs and flows. In the depths of loss, she brings the gift of acceptance and renewal. Embrace her presence as a symbol of resilience. Break free from conventions, for even in the face of adversity, joy and transformation can be found.

*Nothing grieves more deeply or pathetically
than one-half of a great love that isn't meant to be.*
Gregory David Roberts

Six of Cups

*Just waiting for the universe
to give us a sign
Your soul will find me and
merge with mine
It's not a matter of "if";
it's just a matter of "when"
Remember us my love,
until we reunite again*

KEYWORDS & CONCEPTS

LIGHT: nostalgia, creating memories, inner child, friends to lovers, gifts, blast from the past, offer of love, emotionally available, reminiscing, gentle, siblings, protecting the memory of someone, childhood memories, past events, fond memories, meeting with someone from the past, past-life connection

SHADOW: unhappy memories, estranged siblings, past emotional hurt, obsessed with a past lover, stuck in the past, buried memories, childhood hurts, fixated on the past, emotional attachment, dwelling in nostalgia, inappropriate boundaries

Scene The pained look of love on the Dolphin's face strains with desire, as she looks up at the image of her love, the only memento left to remember him by. She heard his soul whispering across the years, "How ever far away you are, I will always find you." She keeps him in her memories and adorned his image with the Six of Cups, regretting the intentional distance she kept so he'd be free. But now he's gone . . . gone for good. Recycled memories have

become the lifeblood sustaining her frigid heart. As she thinks back, she cannot remember their last goodbye, for there were no last words, no last kiss, no last memory captured. Her mind retreats to times when everything was perfect, remembering the days when they were together, young and free. It's those magick nostalgic memories that have helped her get through the days. She cries out in anguish, "I left my heart on the altar of the new life you've built without me." She gingerly touches the three daggers left in her heart, unable to heal but desperately wanting it to beat again.

Every time she tries to move on and carve out a new future, the yellow rubber duck appears with a knowing smirk leading her back into loops of the past, because all roads lead back to him. At night she shares their secrets with the moon, wondering if he's looking up at the same moon tonight. In the pale moonlight, a tear glistens and falls, joining the rest in the salty sea, and she fears she'll never love again. Why did they diverge from the path of destiny, now left living parallel lives? She's become an emotional mess where the past tangles with the present, strangling her heart and refusing to let go, for fear that the memories will go as well. It was in that magickal moment she knew that they will reunite. She whispers into the darkness, "I'm not hard to find, you told me . . . before them there was us." Beseeching the darkness to hear, she shouts into the night, "I am ready for us! Hold on to us. It's always been you at the end of my rainbow, the gift. Come find me; I'm ready."

Six of Cups in Love Honestly reflect, does someone from your past still hold your heart? Do they haunt your dreams, pulling on the strings of your soul? This card signifies an enduring connection, without closure. The pain can feel overwhelming, because soulmates *are* forever.

Six of Cups in Career Returning to work, going back to a previous career inspired by a childhood dream. Working in a scope that evokes nostalgia. This card could also indicate past mistakes made at work, coming to haunt you.

Six of Cups in Wellness Time heals old wounds, but memories remain. Engage in safe conversations to resolve past hurts, particularly those rooted in childhood, fostering true healthful resolution.

Six of Cups in Finances Past financial mistakes have come back to cause havoc, making things much more financially difficult. Let go of things you cannot control, and work on the things you can change, ensuring a better financial future. You will be given a gift, one of great value, but it's up to you what you deem valuable.

The Magick of the Six of Cups The magick lies in the ability to transport you back to cherished memories and evoke the innocence and joy of childhood. Engage in ritual where you revisit a significant place or engage in activities that reconnect you with your inner child. Affirm this: "Through the magick of the past, I embrace joy, innocence, and the abundance of my memories, manifesting happiness in the present."

Words of Wisdom from the Six of Cups If you remember, it was important. Past memories hold significance, yet true freedom lies in letting go.

Spirit Guide—Dolphin The Dolphin, a beloved spirit guide, carries the essence of cherished memories and the innocence of the heart. It beckons you to embrace the beauty of the past, to reconnect with the joy and wonder of childhood. Let the Dolphin's playful nature guide you to a place of innocent love and profound nostalgia, a place where you will always remember them, painless and ageless.

If you remember me, then I don't care if everyone else forgets.
Haruki Murakami

Seven of Cups

*I don't even recognize who
you are anymore
When you left for good,
slamming my door
That day you left me a gift,
when my trust you broke
But it was in that moment
when my soul awoke*

KEYWORDS & CONCEPTS

LIGHT: marvel, amazement, imagination, possibilities, choices, rewards, altered state of consciousness, fantasies, euphoria, visualization, daydreamer, make-believe, utopia, selection, visions, sense of humor, fantasy world

SHADOW: illusions, overwhelmed, mirage, can't choose, giddiness, disbelief, drug- or alcohol-induced high, delusional, pretend, choose wisely, ghosts, confusion, sensory overload, seeing a phantasm, escapism, "it's not what it seems," getting caught up in it all, paranormal activity, disappearing into thin air, wishful thinking

Scene Standing on one leg frozen in place, the Flamingo cannot believe her eyes. What good fortune to see all those wonderful cups lined up before her! She cautiously cranes her long neck to get a closer look at the Seven of Cups, then instantly recoils in the fear that it's all a mirage and will disappear. Blinking rapidly, she arches her eyebrow as a wide smile slowly spreads across her face. She cannot believe her eyes that here on this very night she

stumbles upon a beautiful treasure. She sighs aloud, "This is exactly what I needed!" But her mind wanders lost in thought. How is it that every time she feels the melancholy of life, fearing that things won't get better, something wonderful happens?

"Ribbit, ribbit"; the Flamingo tilts her head to the side where the noise came from. "Oh, hey, frog! Do you see the Seven of Cups over there?" The frog's throat moves rapidly, blowing up bigger and bigger. The Flamingo stares intently, waiting with bated breath to hear that he saw the cups too. Then the frog lets out a long "burp" . . . not the answer the Flamingo hoped to hear. Frowning, now very confused and not sure if the display is real or not, she hasn't moved a muscle. From afar, some would think she's posing like a cup. The frog regards her amusingly, muttering under his breath, "Here's another one that still has yet to learn the secret of the cups," which is—now loudly croaking in her direction—"How you perceive things to be is how they really are." He winks at the Flamingo, letting out another loud "burp," and hops away to another lily pad, to mess with another Flamingo.

Seven of Cups in Love In love, be wary of setting unrealistic fairy-tale expectations within your current relationship. Holding your partner to such standards can hinder the longevity of your shared love. If single, pay attention, since someone is luring you under false pretenses. Remember, sometimes things *are* just too good to be true.

Seven of Cups in Career Keep focusing on your career goals; don't get caught up in workplace drama. Set realistic goals, stay the course, and eventually you'll get where you want to go.

Seven of Cups in Wellness Watch out for tricks of the imagination. The Seven of Cups can be challenging for those with body dysmorphia, by inadvertently skewing their reality.

Seven of Cups in Finances Beware of living in a financial fantasy, maintaining a facade of luxury leading to overwhelming debt. Transparency with finances is crucial. See things as they are, prioritize clarity, make realistic choices, and steer clear of get-rich-quick schemes.

The Magick of the Seven of Cups The magick of the Seven of Cups comes by intuition, sensing beyond ordinary perception. Trust your intuition to discern your energy from others. Precognitive dreaming and signs hold special messages from spirit. Embrace the charm of this card, opening pathways of insight and connection into the beyond.

Words of Wisdom from the Seven of Cups Unveil illusion and behold reality. Seek clarity amid the tempting mirages, for aligned choices that resonate with your psyche will guide you to fulfillment and wisdom.

Spirit Guide—Pink Flamingo The Pink Flamingo, a flamboyant spirit guide, brings the gift of imagination and boundless possibilities. It symbolizes vibrant dreams and creative potential, inviting you to embrace the power of visualization and manifest your deepest desires. Let the Pink Flamingo guide you in the enchanting dance of dreams, where the extraordinary becomes reality.

Love can conquer everything but reality.
Which will win every stinking time.
J. R. Ward

Eight of Cups

*Shadows must be faced,
to truly mend and heal
Broken hearts still beating,
emotions very real
Leaving behind the tears and
unbearable strife
Bravely walking toward the
waiting arms of life*

KEYWORDS & CONCEPTS

LIGHT: acceptance, walking away, leaving painful emotions behind, seeing the light, choosing a course of action, new path, following through, undeterred, moving on, facing your fears alone, putting yourself first, left behind, soul-searching, personal transformation, detaching

SHADOW: leaving alone, abandonment, afraid of the dark, fear of the unknown, no follow-through, fearing change, emotional setback, chasing waterfalls, turning back, feeling alienated, afraid to leave

Scene The Sea Lion casts a final glance at the Eight of Cups, mesmerized by how the last drips of moonlight catch on the bejeweled edges. Just as she was about to turn away, she heard that familiar voice amplifying out of the cups, tempting her, "Please stay. I will change. I'm sorry. I promise things will be better this time." The Sea Lion has been down this road many times before, and each time it never ends well. With a heave of her chest and a heartfelt sigh, she straps her rucksack filled with all her worldly possessions

onto her back. She walks away from the Eight of Cups laden with all her briny tears of spilled hopes, empty promises, paralyzing fears, hurtful words, unpleasant memories, pulverized dreams, and shallow love, and a life of servitude. Compelled by a sudden sense of self-preservation, the Sea Lion quickly swims away, following a sliver of light, in hopes of leaving the strangling darkness behind. Bravely she swims into uncharted territory toward the deep blue abyss, for anywhere is better than staying here in the house of pain.

She's ready for a new adventure as she swims farther away, despite the thick tears gathering in her throat, as darkness creeps into her heart. The farther she swims, the clearer things become, as another path of light magickally forms distinctly in between the shadows ahead. An eerie sound—a siren's song—carried by the undercurrents rises up as she tilts her head toward it. The words quickly find a home in her heart:

Only when you don't look back can you become whole; follow your guiding light into the depths of your soul.

The Sea Lion closes her eyes, inhaling the first crisp breath of freedom as she rises to the surface far away from the bondage of love, vowing to herself that no one will ever stand in her way of greatness again.

Eight of Cups in Love The relationship has run its course; accept the reality and move on. Don't get lost in that last goodbye, just follow your happiness and find your smile again. If single, you're looking for love in all the wrong places, causing more emotional setbacks.

Eight of Cups in Career Lately you may feel uninspired or devalued at your workplace. Time to reevaluate and be open to making changes.

Eight of Cups in Wellness Know your worth in all aspects of life. Release all chaos and clutter, creating inner harmony. Surround yourself with beauty and comfort, quelling the fires within with a blanket of peace.

Eight of Cups in Finances Delve deeply into your finances and assess your position. If you're satisfied with the outcome, kudos for having your financial house in order. If the thought makes you uncomfortable, it's even more reason to do so. Accept your financial situation and bravely chart a course forward, leaving the past behind.

The Magick of the Eight of Cups Even though the final outcome is shrouded in darkness, have the determination to keep moving forward and see it through to the end. There's nothing here for you anymore, in this barren boneyard of broken dreams. Affirm this: "Through the magick moment of the in-between, I embrace the courage to see new future possibilities."

Words of Wisdom from the Eight of Cups Invest wholeheartedly in the eternal abode of your heart, for the foundation built within another's will inevitably crumble, leaving you stranded in the desolate wilderness of profound homelessness. Dare to reclaim your sovereignty and forge an unshakable sanctuary within.

Spirit Guide—Sea Lion The Sea Lion, a spirited and curious guide, brings the gift of forging ahead. It symbolizes the courage to venture out on a soul-searching journey, leaving everything behind. Let the Sea Lion guide you into uncharted waters, embracing the beauty of self-discovery.

One day you will ask me which is more important,
my life or yours. I will say mine, and you will walk away not
knowing that you are my life.
Khalil Gibran

Nine of Cups

In a realm of wishes,
where desires take flight
Nine of Cups overflows with
pleasure and sweet delight
For in the pursuit of pleasure,
one must also beware
The risk of losing oneself
in excess, caught in a snare

KEYWORDS & CONCEPTS

LIGHT: *philotimo*, pleasure, satisfaction, emotional stability, invitation, feast, indulgence, laughter, self-indulgence, comfortable, carnal pleasures, satiated, cravings, gratification, enjoyment, contentment, achievements, agreeable, make a wish!

SHADOW: smugness, overindulgence, inhospitable, greedy, excessive indulgence, slobbish, overemotional, gluttony, instant gratification, starving, using substances to numb the pain, sloppiness, irresponsible, neglect, complacency, unpopular, unfulfilled wishes, emotional imbalance, temporary pleasure

Scene The Dragonfly's wings flutter with excitement as his body undulates with pleasure, mimicking the ripples of the oasis. He intently looks at the alluring Nine of Cups presented before him in awe, craving just one touch. The sound of the lapping waves lulls him into a trance, as vivid visions enter his realm of consciousness. Here in this magickal world, he's content to just

be, with nowhere to go, in the flow, feeling all his senses come alive as this sublime scene unfolds before him. The Dragonfly worked so hard to evolve, growing to the point where he's finally been granted access into the legendary inner sanctum where wishes are granted. From the corner of his eye, he warily glances back at the others who were stopped at the threshold, bringing him right back to the days when he too was not allowed to cross. Suddenly he hears a sweet voice say, "Come forth, little one, and be granted any heartfelt wish you desire."

Immediately lost for words, the Dragonfly's mouth opens and then snaps shut, becoming overwrought with emotion, not being able to think of a single wish. His breath comes in quick and shallow as he struggles to find his voice, his wings fluttering into a nervous blur. The soothing voice eventually quells his panic with words that float around the shimmering strands surrounding the cups. "It's okay, little one. See my rainbow, and all its colors?" The Dragonfly blinks once in silent agreement as the voice continues, "Yes, that's good, little one, very good." Instantaneously the Dragonfly knew what he wanted to wish for, but before he even opened his mouth, the voice spoke again. "I have granted your wish, using all these beautiful colors to take away the turmoil of your soul, by promising a rainbow after every storm." Content, the Dragonfly gently came back to the present moment. Feeling whole and healed, looking into the oasis, he whispers, "Thank you." Then he turns and flies away, determined to share this newfound joy of bringing wishes to others.

Nine of Cups in Love Bask in the overflowing joy of love's fulfillment. Celebrate the union of hearts, indulging in the sweet nectar of emotional satisfaction. Your deepest desires find blissful realization, painting your love story with vibrant hues of pleasure.

Nine of Cups in Career Strive for fulfillment, rejecting complacency's grip. Be cautious of settling for mediocrity, since it breeds discontent. Allow the energy of satisfaction to fuel your professional journey, propelling you toward a rewarding and gratifying career path.

Nine of Cups in Wellness Pay attention to overindulgence, whether it's alcohol, food, or recreational drugs. It's a slippery slope when using substances to numb emotional pain. Unmask your pain by transmuting your troubles into growth, and be mindful what you put into your body.

Nine of Cups in Finances Enjoying your money is one thing, but overindulging and overspending is something else. Focus on finding that sweet spot, where you can spend in a fulfilling, exciting way while keeping your finances in check.

The Magick of the Nine of Cups Traditionally the Nine of Cups is known as the wish card. Go ahead: lay your hands upon this card, close your eyes, and make a wish!

Words of Wisdom from the Nine of Cups Indulge wisely, for abundance masks true contentment.

Spirit Guide—Dragonfly The Dragonfly, a captivating spirit guide, brings the gift of emotional fulfillment. With its iridescent wings, it invites you to embrace gratitude and celebrate the abundance of life. Allow its transformative energy to guide you to where dreams take flight and wishes are realized. Welcome the Dragonfly's wisdom and experience a profound sense of contentment in every aspect of your being.

Too much of a good thing can be wonderful!
May West

Ten of Cups

*The secret to my success was
in the intentions I made
I let go of everything, and the
negativity started to fade
My cups are now filled with love,
and happiness abounds
I've waited so long, finally my happy
ever after I found*

KEYWORDS & CONCEPTS

LIGHT: family, feeling at home, support, soul family, togetherness, sanctuary, promising future, desiring a family, ends well, feeling complete, good times, familiar surrounding, domestic bliss, familial bonds, security, happily ever after

SHADOW: feeling uncomfortable, unconventional family/relationship, superficial happiness, worrying about family, desperate to settle down, unwelcome, unsupportive, emotional chaos, unrealistic dreams, family conflict

Scene On the edge of a grassy bank, Papa Tortoise admires his family frolicking in the shallow waters. He's worked so hard to build this happy life through the bonds they share; puffing his chest out, he says to himself, "This is my happily ever after." He thinks back across the years to all the hardships they've endured and the sacrifices made to get them here, so they can enjoy this beautiful life they've built together. Mamma Tortoise looks over at the children and chuckles to herself, happy that they are just now becoming

better swimmers. She tilts her head toward her mate: "Papa, why don't you put that house down for a minute and come in for a dip? The water is nice and warm, especially around the Ten of Cups, where it's really shallow." Papa Tortoise wrinkles his brow and clears his throat: "I'm good right here; you guys go ahead and enjoy yourselves." Mamma shoots him a knowing glance, her eyes shining with mirth, "Oh, that's right. You don't want the house to get wet. That's it, right?" Papa Tortoise smiles in amusement, slowly nodding in agreement. Mamma smiles at her children when they ask if Papa is coming in today. "Children, you know Papa is watching and keeping us safe, and look at the very important job he has of carrying our house." The children look over at Papa. Seeing for themselves and satisfied with Mamma's answer, they continue to play in the water. Mama Tortoise yells over the splashing, "That's good, children; you've become such good little swimmers!" Looking back at the mossy bank, catching her mate's eye, she adds, "You get that from me!"

She gave Papa a cheeky look and ducked underwater before he could hear her laughter. Shaking her head, she thinks, "Imagine a Tortoise bring afraid of the water . . ."

Ten of Cups in Love Embrace the serenade of true love, where hearts intertwine and souls dance in harmony. A union of deep connection and the possibility of expanding love and family bonds. If single, let connections deepen and familiarity blossom, laying the foundation for a love that lasts.

Ten of Cups in Career The dynamic of your work family has an impact on your daily life, so continue building strong relationship bonds with your work family.

Ten of Cups in Wellness A very fortunate card to see when inquiring about health; enjoy the blessings and let the good times roll! Spend time with loved ones or go visit a relative you haven't seen in a while. All these behaviors are very healthful to the psyche.

Ten of Cups in Finances Your coffers overflow with blessings. Abundance and fortunate opportunities await, elevating your financial status.

The Magick of the Ten of Cups Light a blue candle and let its glow transcend past hurts. With forgiveness and love, ignite a bond that unites family, weaving memories of cherished moments.

Words of Wisdom from the Ten of Cups Let the kaleidoscope of joy paint your world, as laughter dances on the canvas of your heart.

Spirit Guide—Tortoise A wise and ancient spirit guide, it brings the gift of family. The Tortoise embodies the essence of harmonious joy and emotional fulfillment. Like the Tortoise, embrace a steady and patient approach to cultivating loving relationships and creating a harmonious family life. Let the Tortoise remind you to find contentment in the simple pleasures and appreciate the abundance of love and happiness that surrounds you.

What you have told us is rubbish.
The world is really a flat plate supported on the
back of a giant tortoise.
Stephen Hawking

Page of Cups

*I stand and I roar,
so ferocious I can be
Trying so hard to find the
love within me
I trust in others often,
caring way too much
But what I crave is a kind
and loving touch*

KEYWORDS & CONCEPTS

LIGHT: young love, sympathetic, careful, imaginative, sweet, emotionally intelligent, devout, softhearted, psychic, infatuated, sentimental, gentle, hospitable, intuitive flashes, charming, maternal instinct, innocent, fascinated, homebody, good surprise, mamma bear

SHADOW: intense, putting others first, disregards intuition and gut feelings, revengeful, hypersensitivity, trust issues, accommodating to a fault, caretaker, second-guessing yourself, clingy, self-neglect, tough outer shell, crabby, moody, disgruntled, emotionally conflicted, feels unprepared, bad surprise

Scene The Polar Bear intently stares forward, proudly displaying her red cup. As pillowy snowflakes tickle her nose, a satisfied smile slowly spreads across her face. The loving energy of the cup swirls around her, engulfing her aura with a euphoric feeling. For a moment she's totally caught up in all the feels, completely forgetting about the fish, until a subtle splash is heard. Only then does she snap her head toward the sound. Her heart sinks a bit as

she remembers her grandmother's words: "Beware, my child; the fish can be a good or bad surprise. Whatever it be, it won't be expected." Dejectedly, her head falls slightly forward, knowing from experience that most times there's a lesson hiding in the cup. Tipping her head back, she closes her eyes, feeling the moonlight on her face. She mouths the words "I miss you." Straightening her shoulders as a blanket of peace settles over her, she faces the fish, looking it right in the eyes, and says, "I'm ready; give me your best shot." Armed with love and hope in her heart she boldly steps onto the crescent-shaped iceberg, trusting that the tiny skiff will hold her weight, as she pushes off into the watery sea of dreams to seek emotional fulfillment. Startled, the fish suddenly jumps out of the cup and into the frigid water. With a flash of the iridescent scales and a wave of its tail, it disappears into the cold depths. Immediately the Polar Bear's little boat feels lighter, as if a huge weight has been lifted. She dips her cup into the icy water, offering it up toward the heavens, then winks and drinks her fill.

Page of Cups in Love Caught in the abyss of your emotions, where everything has to be felt so deeply, open your heart to whispers of love. Embrace the innocence and vulnerability of new connections, as love's sweet melody begins its enchanting serenade.

Page of Cups in Career Inflexibility becomes a serious problem when having to work in unison with others. Listening to others' ideas and opinions brings value; you are not always right, nor should things always go your way. The Page of Cups is well suited for working alone, behind the scenes and preferably in creative settings.

Page of Cups in Wellness Embrace flexibility in body and mind. Find balance through such practices as yoga to release stress and boost immunity. Let go of preoccupations and flow with the rhythm of life.

Page of Cups in Finances Tap into the imaginative realm of abundance. Seek innovative paths to financial prosperity. Let intuition guide you, unveiling hidden opportunities. Flow with the currents of financial growth, manifesting your dreams into a tangible reality.

The Astrological Sign of the Page of Cups Cancer (June 21–July 22)

Words of Wisdom from the Page of Cups Start romanticizing your life, for relying on others to fill your cup leads to perpetual disappointment.

Spirit Guide—Polar Bear The Polar Bear brings the gift of blending in with your surroundings, in order to gain insight and uncover things hidden in plain sight. When the Polar Bear shows up, this fierce and powerful animal is relentless in guiding you through life's harshest moments. She will teach you how to use the inside knowledge you garnered by encouraging you to never give up until your goal is achieved.

Unconditional love says,
"I'm going to love because I am a lover,
not because you are lovable."
Abraham Hicks

Knight of Cups

*I easily offer my heart,
with a profusion of roses so red
Emotions felt so deeply,
replaying every word I said
With a heart that yearns,
and a gentle soul that seeks
This Knight finds solace in places
where love speaks*

KEYWORDS & CONCEPTS

LIGHT: bringer of messages, communicates through feelings, ruled by the heart, hesitantly moving forward at a slow gait, gentle soul, creative imagination, hopeless romantic, shape-shifter, wears his heart on his sleeve, slow progression, precognitive dreamer, methodical, moving in the right direction, gallant, chance on love, sensitive, flirty

SHADOW: fixated, overzealous, acting out of desperation, trusting, emotionally immature, obsessing over love, imagined affection, philandering, meandering, curveball, idealism, weakness, overemotional, gullible, easily influenced

Scene On a windless night, at the edge of a serene shallow pond, the Knight of Cups is hopeful that this will be the night he gets lucky. Tonight the moonlight is in perfect position, intermittently casting a sheen across the surface of the water, creating a mirrorlike surface. Excited with the prospect of seeing his reflection, the Knight intentionally paces even more quickly, picking up the tempo. His mind drifts to times when his emotions got the

best of him, creating obstacles by standing in his own way of reaching full potential. Following his train of thought further, he seems to find himself often raveled up in the minutia of everything, preventing himself from making any real progress. Frustrated, he snorts loudly, expelling his breath in puffs of clouds that appear in the cool air, as wolves from a distant realm howl in reply, commiserating with his plight. The brisk rhythmic sound of his hooves hitting the mossy bank lures the dragonflies closer to come and see what all the commotion is about. This display of fellowship hijacks his feelings as a newfound emotion settles deeply into his core—that he's never alone.

He finally musters up the courage and gingerly steps into the tepid pool, as the moon casts a beam at precisely the right angle, exploding in a brilliance of sparkles creating the mirrored surface. It's in that moment he realizes that sometimes you just have to be brave enough to take the plunge. At last the Knight looks down into the pool, seeing his image for the first time. He neighs in surprise as an image of a serene majestic beast with soft, expressive, dark eyes peers deeply into his soul, reflecting back to him. Immediately his eyes catch on the beautiful cup on his back, filled with the lushest red roses. A sudden realization comes to him: this is the weightiness he feels. It's all the heavy emotions he carries with him everywhere he goes. The light of the moon shifts and his reflection quickly distorts, fading away. He gives his head a good shake as he slowly trots back up the bank, enlightened.

Knight of Cups in Love This Knight is as sweet as they come. He is ruled by his emotions, and they cause him to hold on to things longer than he should. If single, beware of falling in love too fast. Protect yourself while open to love. If you want to catch this Knight's attention, tread slowly in order not to spook your potential lover.

Knight of Cups in Career The Knight of Cups brings a touch of creativity and emotional depth to the workplace. Welcome passion into your life and let it guide you toward a fulfilling career. If waiting to hear about employment, a message will be coming soon.

Knight of Cups in Wellness Trust your intuition and listen to your body. Nurture your emotional and physical self through creative outlets and deepen your connection to your being.

Knight of Cups in Finances Harness your intuition to explore creative endeavors by embracing your passions to create a prosperous path. Tap into entrepreneurship and find financial success through your imaginative pursuits.

The Movement of the Knight of Cups The Knight of Cups represents aspects associated with water signs. As bringers of messages and the embodiment of pure energy, all Knights are depicted by horses, associated with specific movements, energy, and speed of timing. The Knight of Cups' movement is a trot. He moves along briskly in a lithe manner, bringing messages of love.

Words of Wisdom from the Knight of Cups The Knight of Cups represents aspects associated with water signs. Feel your emotions fully while listening to your intuition. Seek out natural connections since they will point you in the right direction.

Spirit Guide—Orlov Trotter This Russian breed, known for sophistication, was a favorite of the czars. With their artful trot, and slower than most breeds, the Orlov trotter is a determined hardworking horse who steadily keeps moving froward, making progress. When this beautiful gentle giant appears, he reminds you to keep your emotions in check. Let its powerful presence inspire you to steadily move toward your dreams.

A man in passion rides a horse that runs away with him.
Thomas Fuller

Queen of Cups

*How fragile is the heart that desires
to love so deep
Salty, warm, heartfelt tears out
of a leaky chalice seep
Leave behind the veil of fear;
straighten up your crown
No one would dare to try to
hold Her Highness down*

KEYWORDS & CONCEPTS

LIGHT: loving, sensitive, family focused, altruistic, understanding, sexual, empathic, caring, demure, fair, compassionate, clairvoyant, healer, serene, sincere, bonded, committed, purposeful, emotionally in tune, spiritual, intuitive, modest, honest

SHADOW: insecurities, martyr, dramatic, highly sensitive, temperamental, disillusion, unrealistic view, avoiding emotions, insincere, hormonal, promiscuous, secretive, needy, jealousy, easily offended, possessive, overly cautious, abrupt, intimidating, adamant

Scene One night by the light of the moon, the Swan fills her cup brimming with the magickal waters of the wellspring. Comfortably sitting on the edge of the Pond of Inquiry, she nestles into the lush foliage, preparing for another long night. She's been coming here once a month every full moon to seek answers, although tonight feels different, as an eerie quiet hangs on the breath of the wind. The Queen of Cups softly gazes, deeply scrying into her vessel,

mesmerized by the image with dark expressive eyes looking back at her through soft, feathery lashes. Silky aqua tresses are adorned with a bejeweled crown made of pure gold. Dotted with stunning violet roses, its color mimics essence within the cup. A smile slowly spreads over her full ruby-red lips. She ruffles her feathers, for she likes what she sees. Turning her focus back, she redoubles her efforts, staring intently into the cup and focusing on her problem. The more she stares at her image, the more she finds it exceedingly hard to keep her composure. A silky tear slips out of the corner of her eye, falling into the cup and making the slightest "plop." The waters in the cup starts to ripple, and a faint song comes out of the vessel:

> *You will never find the answers you seek without,*
> *for they reside only within.*
> *Reach deeply into your heart; by following your intuition,*
> *life begins.*

Startled by this revelation, the Queen of Cups inadvertently knocks the cup over, marveling as the spilled water quickly runs downward to be once again reunited with its source. Then the Swan notices a slight motion behind her, a whispering of wings; she turns her graceful neck only to see the most beautiful butterfly. With a sharp intake of breath, her chest fills with compassion as she finally finds what she was looking for . . . herself.

Queen of Cups in Love This nurturing Queen possesses an innate ability to make everyone around her feel loved and cherished. When you look into her eyes, you'll see your future, your children, your life. But never take this beauty for granted or you will trigger her vengeful, spiteful side, where anyone and everything is fair game.

Queen of Cups in Career Deeply caring about human plight, this Queen would make an outstanding counselor, therapist, psychic, healer, or nurse, any helper of humanity. In a work setting, she's reliable and very caring toward her coworkers, making her an excellent boss.

Queen of Cups in Wellness Losing touch with reality is the pitfall of this Queen. She becomes so preoccupied with living in a phantasm rather than reality. Being absorbed in her own perceptions leaves her alienated from others, causing a rift in relationships, where she viewed as someone living in her own world. Pay special attention to reproductive organs by getting frequent checkups from a healthcare professional.

Queen of Cups in Finances The Queen of Cups tends to display disdain and animosity toward others whom she deems are financially better off than she. Even with this attitude, she's grateful for what she has or what she gets; the problem is, she's always wanting more.

The Astrological Sign of the Queen of Cups Scorpio (October 23–November 21)

Words of Wisdom from the Queen of Cups Not every romantic connection you experience is meant to evolve into a relationship.

Spirit Guide—Swan The Swan glides into your life, bringing the gift of beauty that lies with and around you. It is a symbol of grace and fortitude, reminding you to cherish your own worth and protect what you hold dear. Let its presence inspire you to embrace you inner beauty, and see the beauty of each soul within all living creatures. The Swan guides you to find harmony between vulnerability and resilience, defending what truly matters with fierce devotion. As sublime as this creature is, once threatened serious injury can ensue, since they will defend anything they value to the death.

> *Someone I loved once gave me a box full of darkness.*
> *It took me years to understand that this, too, was a gift.*
> **Mary Oliver**

King of Cups

In the depths of my heart,
a love for you still thrives
Through the passage of time,
our connection survives
In my dreams I've painted a life
with you, so real
Forever etched in my soul,
the depths of what I feel

KEYWORDS & CONCEPTS

LIGHT: empathy, sixth sense, discernment, sensitivity, self-confidence, authentic, devotion, forgiving, romantic, affectionate, benevolent, bighearted, family man, tolerant, genuine, philanthropist, encouraging, good-natured, sociable, cautious, admiration, shy, dreamer, artistic, mature

SHADOW: complacent, mood swings, passive-aggressive, fickle, doormat, savior, will go to extreme lengths, incognizant, suspicious, oversensitive, very vulnerable, superficial, keeps things to himself, overemotional, insecure, sneaky, resentful, bends over backward for others, complicated

Scene The King of Cups sits at the water's edge on a dark night, as the light of the moon illuminates the golden cup held firmly in his grasp. He's become so engrossed in the way that papery thin dragonfly wings pulse with an auric light that he's forgotten to refill the red vessel before him. Armed with an earnest curiosity, heart fluttering, he sits in his own discomfort, overcome with emotions and mustering up the courage to speak. When the dragonfly comes in for a closer look, the Frog quickly lowers his eyes, choosing to look

down into his cup, for prolonged eye contact always made him feel exposed. Undeterred, the dragonfly dances before the King, beseeching him to look up and be the man befitting the title.

The newly crowned King came here tonight to take what he needs from the Pond of Tall Tales. Tonight's mission was to refill the vessel and take it back to the castle, so whenever he needs he could take a little sip and slip a little white lie. He's become so tired of holding on to every negative word that's spoken, putting too much weight into others' opinions and relying heavily on others' approval for his own emotional well-being. He's so done with all of this emotional turmoil, now physically feeling the ache of weightiness in his chest. The dragonfly once again catches his attention, fluttering her iridescent wings and speaking before he turns away: "Drink now till you're full, my liege, for I will bless you with courage to speak your truth and reign with confidence." He looks quizzically at the beautiful creature, as sudden inspiration blazes wildly in his eyes and touches his soul. This was exactly what he needed, to drink here, using the yellow cup! Filling the chalice directly from the pond and pressing it to his lips, he drinks his fill. Suddenly feeling better, straightening up he looks over at the red vessel, adjusts his golden crown, nods at the dragonfly, and hops away.

King of Cups in Love This King reigns with unwavering devotion, showering his beloved with profound affection. His empathetic nature and deep emotional connection create an oasis of love. But be warned: beneath the tranquil surface lies a fierce protector who will unleash such a storm of vengeance if his trust is shattered. Handle this regal love with the utmost care and cherish the bond forged in the depths of his soul.

King of Cups in Career This King is a compassionate and sensitive boss, creating a work family where empathy and support flourish. He values the personal lives of his employees and offers guidance and flexibility to navigate challenges. Together they create a harmonious and successful work environment.

King of Cups in Wellness The King of Cups, being deeply emotional, may experience gut issues due to intense feelings. Be mindful of holding on to negative emotions, since they can manifest as "dis-ease" in the body.

King of Cups in Finances Emotional intelligence is key when it comes to finances. Take a step back and assess the bigger picture, considering the impact on your financial wellness. Keep your emotions in check when making major financial decisions.

The Astrological Sign of the King of Cups Pisces (February 19–March 20)

Words of Wisdom from the King of Cups Don't compare yourself to others. The only person you are in direct competition with is the person you were yesterday. Embrace your emotions, wield compassion as your sword, and let love be the magick that transforms your world.

Spirit Guide—The Frog The Frog hops into your journey to facilitate a deeper connection with your emotions. Once you fully feel emotions, only then can you decide which ones to keep and which ones need purging. A Frog cannot handle toxic environments, so emulate the Frog and keep swimming out of the murky waters. Eventually you will find a crystal-clear pond with a beautiful water lily waiting just for you.

I think of myself as an intelligent, sensitive human being with the soul of a clown, which always forces me to blow it at the most-important moments.
Jim Morrison

Ace of Swords

*With a glint of silver,
I beckon you to draw near
See your reflection in this blade
that's crystal clear
Take a bold step forward; leave
doubts in the shade
Embrace the truth's strike,
unyielding and unafraid*

KEYWORDS & CONCEPTS

LIGHT: mental clarity, decision, truths, analytical, justice, reason, discernment, air element, positive cut, logical, on point, cutting through illusion, sharp, action oriented, discovery, cutting things out, right

SHADOW: divorce, separation, irrevocable, deadly weapon, pointless, pressure, indecision, confusion, negative cut, tension, blunt, double-edged sword, ruthless, overwhelming, coldhearted, edgy, missing the point, abuse, wrong

Scene The Butterfly awakens from her eternal slumber; time has come to take action and carve out a new beginning by spreading her wings and flying. The silver flash of the blade's razor's edge is her cue to take flight moving on, as she flits off, leaving the struggles of the past behind. She focuses her new eyes, seeing things in a different way, as possibilities unfold around her. Quickly it dawns on her: she's emerged an entirely different creature from last night, when she slept safely in her cocoon. The Butterfly instinctively knows that extreme care must be taken next, for she's precariously close to the truth of her origin, knowing she's right there at the cusp of illusion. After a time of contemplation, she came to the conclusion that she doesn't quite know what she is; she just knows that she's different. Too weary to get closer, as tension builds the Butterfly needs to come to a decision soon, for her first flight has made her tired.

Out of the corner of her eye, she catches a crimson swath of color drawing her in. She laboriously makes her way toward the beautiful display, just missing the sword's point. The Butterfly gets closer to the roses, since the intoxicating aroma of sustenance brought clarity, as how she came to be. First it was a feeling of immense pressure that roused her, as confusion set in, suddenly making her dilemma seem worse. Then instantly she felt herself pulling and separating. No time to think, only to act, as a thick mantle of urgency tugged at her to follow through. Then as the moment arrived, there was no going back. The irrevocable metamorphosis began, and she realizes that the only way out is through. Glinting in her revelation, the Ace of Swords retains its mirrored sheen, tempting many Butterflies over the years with illumination. It beckons them to come in closer for a first look, and to dance a little closer to discovering the truth of knowing who they truly are.

Ace of Swords in Love Love is a battlefield revealing its sharpest weapon, severing ties with a merciless strike. Relationships face sudden change, bringing painful endings and brief encounters. Stay diligent, protect your heart, and seek clarity amid the chaos.

Ace of Swords in Career When the silver sword slashes through, careers tremble and jobs vanish. Among the chaos, gain sharp clarity. Adapt swiftly, for change reveals hidden opportunities, transforming the professional landscape.

Ace of Swords in Wellness The sharp edge of the swords foretells of potential surgical interventions or diagnostic procedures. Handle wounds with care, seek profession guidance, and prioritize healing and recovery.

Ace of Swords in Finances The Ace of Swords ruthlessly severs the ties to inherent wealth, challenging the poverty mentality. Embrace resilience, seek new opportunities, and rise above the limitations of the past. Believe in your ability to rewrite the narrative and manifest financial abundance.

The Magick of the Ace of Swords The Ace of Swords carries the magick to cut through illusions and reveal the radiant truth. Repeat this affirmation when in need: "I harness the might to slice through illusions, revealing the ugly truth. With unwavering clarity, I embrace authenticity's light, severing deceit, and stand in my truth." Remember, the truth hurts, but lies hurt more.

Words of Wisdom from the Ace of Swords Remember, the sword's blade cuts both ways: it defends or wounds. Know that someone's hero is another's villain; it just depends on what side you're on.

Spirit Guide—Butterfly The Butterfly is the quintessential symbol of shape-shifting and transformation. It reminds us that change is inevitable; it will come whether welcomed or not. Resisting change only causes pain, for what you resist persists. With acceptance, it affords you the freedoms of self-expression, allowing you to dance through life, tasting the nectar of flowers with your feet.

My mind's my kingdom.
Francis Quarles

Two of Swords

*Blindfolded in the darkness,
I seek balance and peace
Bounded by my decisions,
uncertainty does not cease
With swords crossed before me,
choices lie in the haze
Finding clarity from within me,
as I navigate life's maze*

KEYWORDS & CONCEPTS

LIGHT: decisions, silence, conflicted, protecting your heart, choices, uncertainty, stalemate, contemplation, opposition, unresolved

SHADOW: denial, cold, hesitant, ignoring, avoiding, crossroads, turning a blind eye, lying to yourself, trapped in your mind, indecisiveness, internal conflict, undecided, refuse to see the problem, head in the sand

Scene The Peregrine Falcon roosts on a petrified, moss-laden wooden limb, contemplating the plight of the soul within the confines of a mortal body. He is confused and in two minds, not wanting to face reality for fear of making the wrong choice and getting hurt. Intent on not letting his emotions influence his thoughts, he uses the Two of Swords as both barrier and protection from heartbreak. After a time of stillness, he faintly hears a voice come from deep within his mind, impressing these words: "Indecisiveness is the eternal enemy of success." Usually priding himself on bravery and purposefulness, he now finds himself mentally blocked and saddened by this stalemate.

Possessing keen eyesight by nature, he shields his senses with a golden helmet, choosing not to rely on anything seen or unseen to aid his thought process. The sharp horns act as a warning, not allowing anyone too close when he's in this state of deep contemplation, and signaling to others to stay back. This purposefully induced darkness enables him to reduce the noise, giving him access to his reasoning mind, curbing both external and internal resistance, thus allowing pure thought to freely stream into his consciousness. Squinting as he turns his attention inward, he is content to sit here as long as necessary in order to move froward in a way of his own choosing, in-line with his soul path to achieve the success he's always dreamed of.

Two of Swords in Love When you shield your eyes and protect your heart, ask yourself what it is that you're refusing to see in your relationship. To gain clarity, find an environment free from distractions for deep contemplation in order to make the tough but necessary decisions about your relationship. If seeking love, release your defenses and embrace openness in the spirit of love.

Two of Swords in Career In the workplace, indecisiveness and lack of transparency disrupt the energy, causing confusion and mistrust. It's important to address conflicts and foster open communication for a healthful and productive work environment. Honesty and clarity will pave the way for positive outcomes.

Two of Swords in Wellness Avoidance and denial of health issues only prolong the healing process. Face the truth of the matter and seek professional guidance. Think through your decisions, putting your well-being first.

Two of Swords in Finances Grasp the truth of your financial situation and see it as an opportunity for positive growth. Take a close look at your spending habits and make intentional changes, no matter how small. Remember that even the tiniest steps can have a profound impact on your pocketbook.

The Magick of the Two of Swords Visualization: Close your eyes and imagine yourself holding two crossed swords across your chest. Uncross them and affirm, "I release indecision, embrace clarity, and make empowered choices. With focused determination, I cut through illusions, finding balance and truth on my path."

Words of Wisdom from the Two of Swords In the tranquil sanctuary of self-reflection, shed the veil of illusions, unraveling the truth that lies within. Embrace the sacred alchemy of discovery as you walk the labyrinth of your being, an eternal soul adorned with mortal flesh. Unleash the symphony of existence, for you are both the artist and the masterpiece, sculpting a life that resonates with timeless perfection.

Spirit Guide—Peregrine Falcon Witness the majestic Falcon, a symbol of duality in flight. Welcome its grace and strength as you navigate the realms of decision-making. With keen vision, discern truth from illusion, finding clarity amid the crossroads. Harness the Peregrine's gift to balance your inner conflicts, vying for control over your emotions. Let the Peregrine lead you through the dance of balance, where choices unfold and balance is restored. Trust your inner compass as you soar, empowered by the spirit of the Falcon. Only when you have mastered this and achieved a state of mental clarity through conscious understanding will you be rewarded with the gift of prowess, to swiftly move through any obstacle or block with precision and great accuracy. For a Peregrine Falcon always hits its mark!

It's a lack of clarity that creates chaos and frustration.
Those emotions are poison to any living goal.
Steve Maraboli

Three of Swords

*The red stain spreading on
my chest, where once my heart
used to be
Badly bleeding and betrayed,
when you broke my heart in three
Tattered ribbons of disappointment,
of all the dreams we've made
Devastated, I wait on the altar of
love for my heartache to fade*

KEYWORDS & CONCEPTS

LIGHT: disappointment, upset, feeling hurt, disheartened, cutting ties with someone, rejection, frustrated, heavy heart, cutting cords, worry in your heart, heartache, dejected, sharp mind, discontentment, free your heart, emotional attachments

SHADOW: brokenhearted, love triangle, inconsolable, shattered, betrayal (relationship), distressed, revenge, pain, sorrow, devastated, stabbed in the heart, mental anguish, emotional trauma, having ill will in your heart, breakup

Scene A hitch caught in the Luzon's coo, as he swallows hard, pressing a wing upon his breastbone, where a piercing agony converged in the center of his chest, the place his heart used to be. Now what remains is just a hollow void permanently marked by a red stain. He whispers, "Everything leaves a mark," especially when the damage is too deep to reach. He lost his mate, his true love. He wasn't ready and she couldn't wait. Reliving the dreams they

made of a life that never happened, as she left him waiting on the altar of forever, with only scars as memories. He wakes up alone to the touch of a cool nest burning with the memory of her.

The Luzon now lives alone in the pits of hell, where she left him to burn with not so much as a backward glance the day she flew away. He shrills in agony into the wind, "I alone love you!" They were just fledglings when they met, starting out in life; she was his future, his everything. Determined to keep looking for her, he waits in this place, willing his heart to heal and become whole again. It's hard to breathe when he thinks of her, muttering to himself, "How did we end here?" Surely he thought his absence would be noticed. Sharp swords slice ribbons of betrayal, disguised like the satiny red leaves he used to wrap her in. Unavoidable emotions rush forth: too devastated, too heartbroken, too shattered, too raw. He feels nothing but numbness, as a stain spreads on his breast where she marked him forever as hers.

Three of Swords in Love Unveils a relentless storm of betrayals and infidelity that stain the once-sacred bond and leave wounds to fester, refusing to heal. Love turns into a tear-stained battlefield, where a trail of broken hearts are left in its wake. Accept the bitter truth: it's over. Take the time and mend your broken heart so it doesn't leave a mark in future relationships.

Three of Swords in Career Brings frustration in the workplace, being passed over for opportunities and feeling disconnected from your job. The daily grind becomes a burden; dragging your feet drains your enthusiasm. It's a sign to reassess your career, seek opportunities that inspire passion, and align with your desires.

Three of Swords in Wellness Go on an inward journey to resolve your pain, for only you hold the power to mend what's broken. Time and introspection are the allies on this path of healing. Pay attention to your heart both physically and energetically, nurturing your heart chakra for restoration and growth.

Three of Swords in Finances Financial disappointments loom, urging exploration for brighter prospects. Seek fulfilling work and diversify your income resources. Remember, true abundance surpasses wealth alone. Embrace your true passion and purpose and thrive.

The Magick of the Three of Swords The Three of Swords invites you to engage in a powerful cord-cutting ritual. Visualize energetic strings connecting you to past hurts or toxic relationships. Affirm your intention to sever these ties as you visualize the Three of Swords cutting and releasing their influence, and reclaim your inner power and freedom to fully experience soulful love.

Words of Wisdom from the Three of Swords The way to love is through pain. Once you understand this, your capacity to love will flourish.

Spirit Guide—Luzon Bleeding-Heart Dove The gentle dove's coos carry a message of healing from profound betrayal. Embrace the heartache and learn from it, for there is a reason for every experience. The Luzon Bleeding-Heart Dove urges you to fully feel your emotions and let them guide you toward growth and soulful love. Remember: don't go chasing fairy tales; stick to the raw and real qualities that mirror the essence of truth.

> *They stood there pretending to be just friends*
> *when all the while everyone in the room could plainly see*
> *that they were only existing for each other.*
> **Emma Blake**

Four of Swords

*Working on my problems,
healing and trying my best
My weary soul finds solace
within a sanctuary of rest
In the stillness of slumber,
I find great respite and peace
Lulled to sleep by a melody,
laden worries find release*

KEYWORDS & CONCEPTS

LIGHT: rest, recuperation, answers are within you, healing, recovery, retreat, hiatus, refuge, do nothing, recharging, time-out, resolving pain, reevaluation, inner dialogue, calming down, inward looking, reflection, rejuvenation, serenity, stillness

SHADOW: resignation, avoidance, falling ill, out of touch, mental illness, disconnection, poor sleep, overwhelmed, feeling cut off, ailments, inertia, mental exhaustion, overthinking, brooding, escapism, unresolved issues, unhealthful detachment, delayed healing

Scene Four Bats hang upside down from ornate swords, each one silently retreating into their minds in hopes of finding solace. The only thing they need now is respite and recuperation, affording them the space to think things through and heal. The swords are meant to weigh them down until the fear breaks, until a point of surrender is achieved. Each Bat tightly curls its inky wings around its body, tucking in its head, trying to make time stop for a moment. That is, all but the Supreme Bat, who stares intently ahead.

She refuses to close her eyes for even a moment, and salty tears land with soft thuds upon her velveteen wings like raindrops hitting a pane. Tired, with scratchy eyes, she too eventually succumbs to the sweet siren's song of her subconscious. She falls into a bittersweet slumber as the glowing disk adorning her third eye keeps watch. On the ground the candle of illumination burns brightly, guiding the Bats into dreamland as they turn their thoughts inward to face their fears and address the warring state of unrest during this period of inertia. The candle's illumination slowly seeps into the dark corners of their minds, bringing about profound healing as new doors of consciousness open up to infinite possibilities. The Supreme Bat survives the sleeping death, gently rousing and coming out of the darkness as she gingerly opens up her eyes, alit with newfound strength. She is ready to face anything as her third eye pulses with magick. The others instantly awaken, spreading their wings and declare in unison, " Long live the Supreme, first of her kind!"

Four of Swords in Love This is a sanctuary for healing after heartache caused by the Three of Swords. Take time to heal what's broken before jumping into another relationship. If already committed, use this valuable time to reevaluate compatibility and alignment of future goals in the relationship.

Four of Swords in Career Take your full lunch, take those breaks, and take vacation time. Don't answer the phone or messages when you're on personal time. It's important not to be accessible 24/7. You come first, and a job is just something you do.

Four of Swords in Wellness A healing sanctuary, a haven for recovery and restoration. It invites you to focus on finding solace in the stillness. Embrace this period of rest, allowing your body, mind, and spirit to rejuvenate and heal.

Four of Swords in Finances Enter a period of financial respite and take a break from spending, turning your thoughts toward saving. Use this time of calm reflection to fortify your resources, to ensure an abundant future.

The Magick of the Four of Swords The Supreme Bat adorns her brow with a disk of cinnabar, accepting the transformative power of this stone. It brings mental clarity, shifting your perspective to the depths of your soul. Hold the cinnabar close and allow this transformative stone to work its magick.

Words of Wisdom from the Four of Swords When the world falls away and you are left with your own thoughts, listen carefully to that small voice; it knows things.

Spirit Guide—Bat The Bat swoops into your life, asking you to face your fears and embrace growth. In the depths of darkness, profound healing unfolds. Embrace life's challenges as catalysts for change. Awaken from slumber, emerging from the shadows into the light, for anything that grows needs to feel the light.

> *To the mind that is still, the whole universe surrenders.*
> **Lao Tzu**

Five of Swords

*In the aftermath of battle,
I stand with weary eyes
The taste of bitter victory,
hollow echoes in my cries
Lost in the shadows of shattered
honor and broken swords
A price too high to pay, for the
hostile triumph's rewards*

KEYWORDS & CONCEPTS

LIGHT: conflict resolution, strategic thinking, triumph, battle of wits, differences, clashing views, conviction, taking sides, inner struggle, turmoil, dilemma, growing through conflict

SHADOW: conflict escalation, battle, aggression, adversity, manipulation, damaging relationships, abusive, division, outward struggle, vicious, uprising, ego-driven actions, hostility, repercussions, infighting, hurtful words

Scene The Seagull, bearing the battle scars of war, fights over a few scraps. This fighting has becoming increasingly imperative nowadays for daily survival. When he comes across something he wants, he must battle the flock, laying claim to the tiniest morsel by loudly squawking, "MINE!" But today's victory is different. He's scored something so big that he's the envy of all as he puffs up with pride, perching on the edge of the wooden cask and staking his claim. The Seagull sharply thrusts his beak upward, eyeballing the others circling in the sky, daring them to come down and challenge him for it. The others observe the menacing stance of the self-proclaimed victor and see the glint in his eye, and, feeling the seething glare from below, they watch as he confidently claims his prize. This behavior doesn't overly concern the others, for they're smart enough to know that you can't win every fight. But knowing when to retreat in order to live and fight another day is priceless. The Seagull wears the spoils in his hat, preening his crown of glory purposefully in view of the others while staking the fifth sword before him as a visual act of intimidation. Now he's become one of the fringe minority; he's taken a stance, severing all ties to the flock. The only thing left now is a division line, with them on one side and him on another.

Five of Swords in Love Reconsider your battles, for emotional scraps hold no value. Conflict in relationships may reveal deeper issues. It's time to address the reality of your "situationship" and let go of the defensiveness. Open your heart to love by releasing the urge to fight.

Five of Swords in Career Represents communication in the workplace, any conversations taking place. Focus on effective communication with coworkers because words can be pointy little daggers, so be mindful.

Five of Swords in Wellness When someone shuts down and stops communicating, it traps unspoken emotions wreaking havoc on the body. As a result, the body is weakened in fighting off diseases, setting the immune system into overdrive, battling to regain harmony.

Five of Swords in Finances This card typically arises in situations where family members engage in legal disputes over inheritances, leading to deep division between members. Remember, when fighting over money, the only things you lose are money and family.

The Magick of the Five of Swords Shift your focus from the negatives and see the light within any situation. Celebrate each step toward resolution, for even the smallest victories accumulate, tilting the scales in your favor, making way to triumph over adversity. Affirm this: "I release negativity and embrace growth. Each step forward brings me closer to victory."

Words of Wisdom from the Five of Swords Like the Seagull, sometimes you have to eat garbage first, so you can appreciate what filet mignon and caviar taste like. The struggle is real!

Spirit Guide—Seagull Ruling over the elements of water, air, and earth, the Seagull is equally comfortable in each domain. Known as shorebirds, never venturing too far off land, they prefer the mystical space of where the element of water blends with elemental earth, surrounded by air. Gulls are masters at communication, effortlessly reading the subtleties of vocal tones and body language. When the Seagull glides into your life, he brings the gift of observance. Pay attention to nuances of words, revealing a different picture than what is being insinuated.

> *Tragedy and adversary are the stones we sharpen our swords against so we can fight new battles.*
> **Sherrilyn Kenyon**

Six of Swords

*I depart of my own accord,
bidding this shore goodbye
My destination unknown,
I have no more tears to cry
Seeking refuge for my soul,
a sanctuary to moor my boat
Salty tears are my only
companion, and keeping
me afloat*

KEYWORDS & CONCEPTS

LIGHT: physical distance, transition, letting go the past, healing, travel overwater, pivoting, departure, long distance, progression, goodbye, guidance, troubleshooting, vantage, self-improvement, accountability, inner journey, autonomy, calmness, better shores, acceptance

SHADOW: leaving with others, evasive, the ferryman, bailing, turbulence, head trip, emotional baggage, travel delays, escape route, resistant to change, running away from problems, taking the kids, fear of the unknown, denial, unresolved conflicts

Scene The hallowed silence continues, and the only sound heard is the gentle waddling of the Canada Goose carrying her precious cargo nestled between her downy shoulders. Her body prickles with unease as she leans away from the night's sinister shadow appearing on her left. Taking three deep breaths, she melds even deeper into the foreboding night, turning her attention toward the glow of the reflective moon and trusting it to show her the way. With every step forward, she feels her dreams crumble beneath her, just like the carpet of daisies unintentionally being crushed underfoot. She doesn't try to hold on to anything anymore; she exhales, letting everything fall away like the innocent petals scattering in the wind.

Silhouetted against the moon, she sees six of her kind flying wild and free. An envious scream bubbles up into her throat, looking for release. Faltering, she second-guesses her next step as memories of the past flash unwanted images, flooding her boat of consciousness, reminding her that in life there's no guarantee of happiness. Having learned this lesson all too well, she continues to wear her veil as a reminder, vowing never to forget. Determined to get away, thrusting out her chest, she continues lumbering along, with safety being her only goal. The next tentative step takes her onto a path carved out by the Six of Swords, urging her onward and carrying her farther away from the strife and struggles of the past. Unsure of her final destination, she intentionally keeps moving toward her future, in hopes of finding better. As the wind picks up, ruffling her feathers and propelling her onward, another gust whips around, howling in her ears. She swears she just heard it say, "Don't look back."

Six of Swords in Love Gently paddle away from toxic shores, leaving behind the pain that haunts your heart. Seek clarity in relationships. Discern truth from illusion. Single? Embark on a voyage of self-discovery, finding love in the depths of your being.

Six of Swords in Career Embark on a journey toward a fulfilling career. Plan your exit strategy from a dead-end job and seek new opportunities. Don't settle for comfort over growth. Welcome the winds of change and trust that the path ahead will lead to brighter horizons.

Six of Swords in Wellness Focus on healing past traumas and setting your sights toward recovery. You've carried the wounds of these heavy swords for far too long; it's time to heal. If you're struggling, the appearance of the Six of Swords is indicative of something leaving your life.

Six of Swords in Finances Release the chains that bind you in financial situations. Dare to step into the unknown, for within the currents of change lie hidden opportunities. Embrace the courage to carve out a new path, where abundance and fulfillment await your arrival.

The Magick of the Six of Swords On a windy day, harness the transformative power within you, for in every storm lies the opportunity for growth. Embrace resilience as your superpower and rewrite your story with unwavering determination and a spirit that knows no bounds.

Words of Wisdom from the Six of Swords Amid turbulent tides, find solace in the boat of serenity, guided by unseen hands toward new shores of healing and hope.

Spirit Guide—Canada Goose The Canada Goose gracefully glides into your path, embodying big-picture vision and patriotism. Witness the power of synchronized flight, a symphony of wings and honks, as each goose contributes to the whole. Embrace your autonomy in this journey of liberation. "Honk, honk" your heart's melody, resonating with the chorus of shared growth and transformative possibilities. Together, let us soar fearlessly, united in purpose and enjoying the harmonious cadence of the collective.

Once you make a decision to move on, don't look back.
Your destiny will never be found in the rearview mirror.
Mandy Hale

Seven of Swords

"Come into to my parlor"
was the last thing he heard
She wrapped him up so tightly,
manipulated by words
Pretty temptress tricked him,
promise of a big surprise
A fatal mistake he made,
which led to an untimely
demise

KEYWORDS & CONCEPTS

LIGHT: strategy, cunning, stealth, resourcefulness, reclaim, mental acuity, agility, cleverness, salvage, recycle, stolen, self-preservation, retrieve, avoiding confrontation, cutting your losses, eagerness

SHADOW: cheater, sneaky, conspiracy, underhanded, lies, agenda, spying, opportunist, Machiavellian, theft, deceptive, multiple issues, calculated, scheming, stealthy, greed, stalker, betrayal, guilt, lack of trust

Scene The Black Widow took care to meticulously spin her web of lies, incorporating seven razor-sharp swords she stole from a nearby battlefield, arming herself with more than just poison. She continues to methodically lay her trap, and her lips curve into a mischievous smile as she touches her velvety tongue to a fang, drawing a droplet of blood, savoring the flavor in anticipation. "Will you walk into my parlor?" said the Spider in a husky voice. She welcomed her prey wearing only a smile and pearls, committed to her guise of femme fatale, living for the thrill of the game.

Flashing her undercarriage, her crimson hourglass draws the curious prey closer, as she shoots out a fine silky thread promising the raptures of bondage. The profuse perfume of roses and the smell of sexual excitement hang in the air, mesmerizing her prey as he comes even closer, breathless but hesitant. She bats her eyelashes slowly, turning away and feigning boredom. Suddenly becoming more intrigued, the prey leans forward and begins following the black beauty deeper into her parlor. The Black Widow suddenly feels the telltale vibrations of a struggle reverberating through the web. She sharply turns around, drooling as she approaches her prize. Their eyes meet as she sees the unmistakable realization reflected in his eyes. She licks her ruby-red lips and breathlessly finishes saying, "'Tis the prettiest little parlor that ever you did spy."

Seven of Swords in Love Love's battlefield is riddled with deceit and betrayal. Be vigilant, trust your intuition, and be on the lookout for suspicious behaviors. Seek authentic connections rooted in mutual respect and transparency.

Seven of Swords in Career Approach the workplace with caution. Beware of deceit, half-truths, backstabbing, and hidden agendas. Keep your integrity intact and protect your interests. Stay vigilant, since the game is afoot. Trust your instincts and protect your reputation.

Seven of Swords in Wellness Listen to the signals of your body, for they hold the key to restoration. This card is indicative of multiple issues. If you're feeling off, go and get it checked out. Letting issues pile up just creates bigger messes.

Seven of Swords in Finances Sharpen your financial senses, discerning the true gems amid illusions. Guard against cunning schemes and embrace calculated risks. Trust your instincts as a vigilant guardian of wealth, ensuring prosperity and thwarting deceit.

The Magick of the Seven of Swords Unleash the alchemy of preparedness, where anticipation meets surrender. Within this potent space, magick manifests and destiny unfolds.

Words of Wisdom from the Seven of Swords In the intricate web of your mind, stories take shape. Rewrite the narrative within, and witness the magick that transforms your external reality.

Spirit Guide—Black Widow Spider Weaver of mysteries and keeper of magick, the Black Widow has emerged as your guide. You are the protagonist of your story, the orchestrator of your destiny. Be like the Spider: she sits in the heart of her labyrinth after creating a web of possibilities, patiently awaiting what comes her way. Effort, expectation, and patience are the magickal ingredients that will lead you to success. Embrace your role in the labyrinth of life and watch the magic unfold around you.

> *When the spider would attack thee,*
> *it extends its web to entangle thee.*
> **Sir Richard Francis Burton**

Eight of Swords

*The melody of my soul haunts me;
notes taste bittersweet
Safe boundaries I create,
keeping away others in retreat
Waiting for a Knight's rescue,
playing the damsel in distress
Relying on others to save me is
making my life a bigger mess*

KEYWORDS & CONCEPTS

LIGHT: personal boundaries, safety, overthinking, waiting to be rescued, helplessness, allowing your problems to define you, playing victim, not wanting to face problems, self-imposed, feeling trapped in your circumstance, thinking to break free

SHADOW: unapproachable, feeling trapped, barricaded, limited beliefs, mentally blocked, self-sabotage, restrictions, ensnared, overwhelmed with problems, blocked energy, damsel in distress, fearing vulnerability, incarceration, victim mentality, entrapment, paralyzed by fear

Scene The crestfallen head of the Yellow Canary hangs even lower, ensnared by his own paralyzing thoughts while helplessly clinging to his perch. The inability to release the mind from the clutches of terror gives him a skewed vision of reality, as he remains fixated on the boundary created by the Eight of Swords. All he desires is the freedom to fly at will and sing once again, but all he feels is the weightiness of the rusted chains hanging above his head. They hold him down as he struggles to take another shallow breath.

He opens his mouth and clears his throat, and nothing. There is no music; only the song of a strangled cry of frustration escapes. A slight shiver racks his body as the realization hits: he's stuck and has become a prisoner of his own mind. The shine of the pointy swords is the only thing dominating his line of sight. Pausing, he tilts his head, getting lost in the fantasy of his tragic death. "So, this is it. If I fly, I die. This is the cost of my freedom!" Frustrated, he beseeches the swords. Suddenly a flash of an orb catches the corner of his eye. Turning his head slowly, seeking out the source, he sees salvation in the gilded door of his jailer. Shaking his head, for surely his eyes are playing tricks on him, the door seems to be ajar. He blinks rapidly as his eyes nervously move around the cage, torn between the safety of the cage and the freedom of flight. Frozen in indecision, sadly the Canary realizes that both realities cannot simultaneously exist. He succumbs to remaining tethered to the safety of his cage, convincing himself of the comforts of home, while the quiet voice inside him screams, "Freedom!"

Eight of Swords in Love Putting up barriers out of fear of vulnerability is common for those deeply hurt in the past. Lay down your swords, overcome negative assumptions, and embrace love. If single, be mindful of self-sabotage from fear of getting hurt. Avoid being caught in the trap of becoming someone's possession.

Eight of Swords in Career Break free from the confining cage of your job and soar to extraordinary heights. Welcome workplace challenges as stepping-stones to growth. Beware of whispered rumors, since a trusted coworker is singing like a canary.

Eight of Swords in Wellness Falling into the guise of victimhood will create only more mental heath issues resulting in physical problems. Things fester by inaction, so get moving and stop being imprisoned in your mental cage. Begin listening to that little voice that starts a sentence with the words "I will."

Eight of Swords in Finances Feeling trapped by financial limitations and choosing to ignore the problem rather than attempting to fix it leads to a road to utter ruin. Challenge yourself to face the facts by scrutinizing your finances; encourage yourself to come up with an actionable solution.

The Magick of the Eight of Swords The magick of the octave; let music be the lifeblood of the soul; liberate your spirit. Find healing through sound therapy and raise your voice to new heights.

Words of Wisdom from the Eight of Swords A victim is created the moment the mind accepts a label to be true, confining you to live out your days in a prison, where all you see are the bars of the cage. Trapped and living like a prisoner, wherein you are your own jailer.

Spirit Guide—Canary The sweet song of the Canary brings the gift of using the power of your voice. Let your song bring healing and harmony in every interaction. Use the sweet tones to speak your truth in every conversation, especially the ones you have with yourself, because words have a way of keeping you caged.

I started to build a home with all the walls
I was putting up for myself, but when I was finished,
I realized I had built a cage and didn't make a key.
Lidia Longorio

Nine of Swords

*In the darkness of night,
my soul sheds silent tears
Anxiety coils around me,
manifesting all my fears
Nightmares claw at my mind,
tormenting my sleep
With shadows of despair,
and the secrets they keep*

KEYWORDS & CONCEPTS

LIGHT: anxiety, worries, bad dreams, stress, uneasy, inner demons, troubled, heavy mind, disruptive thoughts, fretful, realizations, embarrassed, miserable, distraught, feeling sorry for yourself, sleepless nights

SHADOW: guilt, torment, panic attacks, sobbing, nightmares, depression, anguish, shame and humiliation, distress, overwrought, traumatized, delusion, suffering, disturbed, broken, alone, obsessive thoughts, insomnia

Scene At 3 a.m., a panic-fueled flight of terror spurred this little mouse into leaping out of bed, screaming, "Monsters are real!" Stark terror flashes in his eyes, realizing that the monster under the bed has come out and is now towering over him. At first he thought this to be a nightmare, but waves of nausea told him otherwise, as a cloud of the creature's rotted breath came rolling out of a gaping mouth lined with yellowed razor-sharp teeth. Profusely pinching his nose and holding his breath offered very little protection from the ghastly stink. The little mouse felt hot tears of fear roll down his cheeks,

as the Shoebill's menacing yellow eyes stared at him like a midnight snack. Through his wispy lashes, the mouse looked to the Nine of Swords lining the top of the creature's head like a murderous mohawk. Racked with sobs, he cries, "As if your face isn't scary enough! Really?"

Covering his eyes, he is unable to hold it together. Feeling the pieces of his fragmented mind slip through his fingertips, he thinks this can't be real, as the monster's silhouette continues to dance in the shadows of his mind. Words of worthlessness whispered repeatedly by the Shoebill's chilling voice brought him to his knees on the altar of desperation, as strangled gulps of anxiety engulf him, swallowing him whole. These were his last conscious thoughts before the lights went out, and then silence, as little mouse succumbed to the darkness within.

Nine of Swords in Love Dark shadows haunt the realm of love, suffocation with anxiety and relentless worry. Wake up from the nightmare of overthinking, seek solace in vulnerability, and embrace the healing power of open communication and transparency. Rise above the torment and let love conquer fear.

Nine of Swords in Career You're ensnared in the suffocating grip of work demands, and copious amounts of tasks and responsibilities have been placed on your shoulders. Each day begins to feel like an endless loop, draining your vitality and eroding your spirit. Use this darkness as a catapult for change. Break through the fear and know your worth.

Nine of Swords in Wellness Mental suffering, anxiety, and depression coupled with many sleepless nights are the effects of the Nine of Swords. Sleep is very important for the body's natural rhythms, for healing of the mind, and for rejuvenation of the spirit. So make sure you are getting high-quality rest.

Nine of Swords in Finances In the relentless grip of financial woes, sleep becomes a distant memory. But worry alone won't wake you up from this nightmare. Time for action! Take hold of the key to change and the potential for success. With hard work and an abundant mindset, watch as the universe aligns to manifest your financial goals.

The Magick of the Nine of Swords The Nine of Swords demonstrates the power of the mind. Once you fixate on something and perceive it to be factual or real, it will be only a matter of time until that very thing materializes. Use caution where your thoughts and mind rest, making sure you're always focusing on the best possible scenarios.

Words of Wisdom from the Nine of Swords "I am as real as you want me to be. Imagine something different if you don't like what you see."

Spirit Guide—Shoebill The Shoebill emerges as a symbol of resilience and inner strength, guiding you though the challenges represented by the Nine of Swords. With its prehistoric appearance, the Shoebill teaches you to tap into ancient wisdom and find the courage to rise above fear. Like the Shoebill, you have the power to float above your troubles and take a breather. Trust in your innate ability to buoyantly rise above the darkness through the power of transmutation.

Thoughts are tyrants that return again and again to torment us.
Emily Brontë, *Wuthering Heights*

Ten of Swords

*In the grip of shadows,
a demon's treachery creeps
Disguised as an angel, innocence
cunningly she keeps
With a wicked smile, her blade
gleams with malice and scorn
Unrelenting stabs, a merciless
dance out of darkness reborn*

KEYWORDS & CONCEPTS

LIGHT: endings, collapse, back pain, acceptance, letdown, giving up, precarious position, discomfort, mislead, dismay, receiving a blow, nothing left

SHADOW: betrayal, overpowered, backstabbed, deadweight, shock, murder, treachery, double-crossed, attacked, stabbed, cutthroat, defeat, painful ending, powerless, unsuccessful outcome, it's done, frenemies

Scene The blow overpowered the little Blackbird as she fell from the sky and collapsed, her crumpled posterior on the earthen floor in a heap. She was stabbed in the back and left to die utterly alone. The betrayal came quickly under the cover of night; a cowardly strike that sent her hurtling toward the ground with an audible thud of deadweight. Before vanishing into the inky night, the coward pinned her to the earth with the pointy tips of the Ten of Swords, making sure she would never fly again. The last conscious thought that trickled through her mind before the darkness came was "I was so gullible, and weak, such an easy target."

Lying there and counting down the final thuds of her heart, she watched streams of pleasant memories cross her mind; the last memories were of her life, her family, her loves, bringing a bit of warmth to her cold flesh. The weighty lids of her eyes refused to open when she felt a presence watching over her. Alarmed, she fought to stay calm and collected. Abruptly a sound was heard just over the din of the whipping wind, piercing the silence as a darkness hung, suspended by time. Straining to hear, the little Blackbird reached out with the last shred of consciousness, to no avail, thinking it's probably just the keening of the wind harmonizing with the agony of her soul. Then once again, the same sound knocked on the door of her consciousness, louder this time. She heard a voice right by her ear say, "Get up!" Then even louder, "GET UP!" The source seemed to be coming from the statue behind her. Finding her last drop of strength, she tried to move her wings, remembering how good it felt to soar free in the endless skies. Try as she might, she ended with defeat as the last bits of energy left her body. She could feel the coolness of the stone arms raise her up into the air, giving her over to the light to take her the rest of the way home.

Ten of Swords in Love The most heartfelt betrayal is when it comes from someone whom you loved and trusted. The relationship will end; stop getting lost in the illusion and expending futile energy. Accept that it's the closing of a chapter, and end of an era. If looking for love, now is not the time, for this is a card of endings.

Ten of Swords in Career Be wary of coworkers or management who are quick to throw you under the bus. Betrayal comes with many faces and in many guises. Be on the lookout for someone in your midst who doesn't have your best interests at heart. This card can also speak of a job or career coming to an end, after many years of employment.

Ten of Swords in Wellness This card denotes pain associated with the spine or back area. Stiffness, sciatica, or numbness in the limbs all are relevant to the Ten of Swords. Try acupuncture to relieve nerve pain and stiffness and to relax the muscles.

Ten of Swords in Finances The sharp sting of financial betrayal pierces deep, leaving wounds of loss and broken trust. Guard your resources freely, for deceit lurks in familiar faces. Take heed, settle debts, and rebuild your financial fortress.

The Magick of the Ten of Swords The Ten of Swords is here to mark a natural ending to a chapter of your life. When the pits of darkness swallow you whole, bringing you to your knees, muster the courage to choose a new path and keep moving toward the light. Affirm this: "From darkness, I emerge stronger. For the shattered pieces give birth to my breakthrough."

Words of Wisdom from the Ten of Swords In the stabbing depths of pain lies the fertile ground for the soul's rebirth, as wounds become wings.

Spirit Guide—Blackbird In the depths of despair, the Blackbird emerges as a beacon of hope. With wings of resilience and a lament of transformation, it guides you through the shadows. Embrace the gifts of release and surrender, for they pave the path to rebirth. Let the Blackbird's melody ignite your spirit, inspiring you to transcend limitations and rise anew. Fan the ember within, for even amid the ashes of chaos, your wings can carry you toward the light.

You may shoot me with your words, you may cut me with your eyes, you may kill me with your hatefulness, but still, like air, I'll rise!
Maya Angelou

Page of Swords

*In the realm of airy thoughts,
poignant memories remain
Holding on to every harsh word
etched, deeply ingrained
I'm known to be amusing, hiding
deep hurts behind a joke
Appearing happy on the outside,
while on bitter tears I choke*

KEYWORDS & CONCEPTS

LIGHT: agile mind, naturally curious, funny, happy-go-lucky, chatty, energetic, easygoing, youthful, communicative, decisive, multitasking, always on the go, joker, social butterfly, inquisitive, sensitive, investigative

SHADOW: inappropriate, gossipy, inconsistent, nervous laugh, Jekyll and Hyde, nosy, touchy, uncaring, sarcastic, calculating mind, flighty, exaggerator, untrustworthy, overthinker, white lies, "Jack of all trades, master of none"

Scene The Dove climbs the air toward the highest realms, thinking to himself, "What could I have done so wrong, to lose favor with the gods?" He redoubles his efforts to get there quickly, knowing that summonings are never good, when sheets of music begin to rain in the sky, leaving a trail of notes to follow into the upper sanctums. Upon arrival, he's led through gilded doors into a chamber. He sees a fancy outfit laid out upon a throne with a note. Following the instructions, he dons the costume, consisting of a magick

hat to protect his mind from being negatively influenced, a ruff collar symbolizing aristocracy, and a sword he instinctively takes up in his clutch. Immediately booming throughout the marbled halls, the one voice of the gods states, "From this time forward, you will forever be known as the Page of Swords."

The Dove steps forward with widespread wings, accepting his new title wholeheartedly, as he embraces the heavens one last time before leaving as Page of music, sent forth to share this gift with the realm below. Using the magickal sword, he tears a slit in the fabric of time, slipping through and appearing back in the human world. The Dove's thoughts turn inward, curious as to how beings in the lower world ever survived this long without music, for frequencies and vibrations hold the universe together. Feeling sadness for the humans below, the Dove spreads his glorious wings once again, and this time, sheets of music fly out in every direction, to every corner of the world, raining inspiration with the gift of song to all willing to listen.

Page of Swords in Love This Page has commitment issues, always investigating the grass on the other side, for fear of missing out. As a partner, don't try to tie him down too early in the relationship, for he will abruptly run the other way, leaving you wondering what just happened.

Page of Swords in Career Everyone has known a Page of Swords in the workplace. He's the guy who gets along with everyone, but no one *really* knows him. He's the guy everyone picks to be on their team for fun activities, but when it *really* counts, he's the one picked last. You can count on him, but not when it *really* counts. That's the Page of Swords; he's that guy.

Page of Swords in Wellness When this card shows up, it can be indicative of minor surgery. This Page is susceptible to the cold, so take care to protect hands and feet to avoid chills and developing Raynaud's phenomenon. Watch for respiratory issues such as asthma, coughs, colds, flus, and allergies.

Page of Swords in Finances The Page of Swords' motto is "I think," since he wields a sharp mind when it comes to finance. Unleash your intellectual swordplay, strategize with persuasion, and conquer monetary goals. The key here is to embrace your visionary spirit and have a road map in place, enabling you to see the clearest path to achieving your goals.

The Astrological Sign of the Page of Swords Gemini (May 21–June 20)

Words of Wisdom from the Page of Swords As an overthinker, I need clear communications with all my interactions. Only then can I get out of my head and feel my heart.

Spirit Guide—White Dove This ethereal creature brings tendrils of peace to all that open their hearts desiring serenity. When a White Dove appears, it's a sign to make peace, first with yourself and then with others. Understanding forgiveness gives you wings to fly free.

> *Music is the language of the spirit.*
> *It opens the secret of life, bringing peace, abolishing strife.*
> **Kahlil Gibran**

Knight of Swords

Swiftly delivering tidings while staying the course
Bearing the message, devoid of empathy or remorse
No filter in my speech; words wildly fly and spread
Meeting silence and stares, must be something I said

KEYWORDS & CONCEPTS

LIGHT: bringer of messages, communicates through actions, ruled by the mind, going for it, rapid movements, action oriented, swiftly moving forward, quick on his feet, giver (go hard), speedy, clumsiness, hastiness, excitement, quick-witted, life of the party

SHADOW: daredevil, impulsive, frantic, accident prone, disarray, mistakes, going too fast, hyperactivity, rowdy, devil-may-care attitude, disorderly, going against the grain, inexhaustible energy, elusive, doesn't think before he speaks

Scene Chasing the wind as it whips through the silky, gray-streaked mane of the Knight of Swords, his hooves hit the frosty ground with determination, urging him to gallop even faster. His heart is beating out of his chest, and his immediate instinct is to trample anything in his path that prevents him from reaching his goal, since he's that intent to succeed. Powerful hindquarters propel him forward as he intensifies his speed, redoubling his effort.

In a moment's notice, he stops and stretches his neck to smell the air. He changes his mind and direction in a flash, as a newfound resolve settles within his mind. Charging the wind, yelling, "I made up my mind; I won't change it! Do you hear me?" He's satisfied to release a bit of steam back to its source, continuing on with his course of action, because once he gets something in his head, there's no deterring him. This thought unnaturally stops him in his tracks, catching his breath he exhales, "But I'm always in my head." The blueish light of the moon hits the woods in a way that catches the eyes of the Knight as he energetically blasts forward. He's breathless once again from exertion, as frosty wisps of air escape from his nostrils, turning into intricate snowflakes as unique as him. With a renewed burst of energy, he careens into the opposite direction, taking off once again.

Knight of Swords in Love This Knight brings fleeting passion, an exhilarating whirlwind. Brace yourself for a thrilling encounter, but beware of his restless spirit. Commitment is not his forte, so seek lasting love elsewhere. Chasing a Knight who can't stand still leads to a path of unfulfilled desires.

Knight of Swords in Career Charges into dynamic careers, fearlessly embracing physical challenges. His words cut through barriers, fueling progress with his innovative ideas. In fast-paced workplaces, he is the energy driving success, while his daring spirit inspires other to break barriers and achieve greatness.

Knight of Swords in Wellness This Knight's impulsiveness and lack of attention to detail make him clumsy and prone to accidents. Hyperactivity is common for this Knight, since he's ruled by the mind and rushes headlong into situations without considering safety, leading to precarious circumstances.

Knight of Swords in Finances The Knight of Swords loves charging things on credit, often resulting in overspending. Being drawn to a fast lifestyle and indulging in extravagant living usually lead to rapidly depleting finances. This card denotes money leaving at a quicker rate than it can be replenished.

The Movement of the Knight of Swords The Knight of Swords represents aspects associated with air signs. As bringers of messages, and the embodiment of pure energy, all Knights are depicted by horses, associated with specific movements, energy, and speed of timing. This is the fastest Knight of the deck; he is galloping at a high speed. When the Knight of Swords shows up in a reading, it predicts fast timing and things happening very quickly or coming soon. He brings a message of warning.

Words of Wisdom from the Knight of Swords Unleash the Knight's swift prowess, slashing through barriers. With courage, voice your ideas, igniting a revolution. Embrace the exhilaration of charting your own course, for extraordinary achievements await those who dare to defy convention.

Spirit Guide—Arabian Horse The Arabian is known for its eloquence and speed, here to remind you to take pause and process your thoughts before blurting them aloud. Embrace your quickness, whether it be movement or wit, but have the wisdom to know when to slow down. Channel that incredible endurance and versatility to help you carry your goals into fruition. The Arabian needs constant mental stimulation, just like the Knight of Swords, or it will get bored and take off, usually in the wrong direction.

He flung himself from the room,
flung himself upon his horse, and rode madly off in all directions.
Stephen Leacock

Queen of Swords

*Be prepared when I summon you,
with a look, not a call
Dare look me in the eye,
if you think you have the gall
Cross me once and you'll remember
never to do it again
That's why I'm the Queen of Swords,
forever will I reign*

KEYWORDS & CONCEPTS

LIGHT: diplomatic, tactful, peacemaker, elusive, mediator, logical, active, sociable only on their terms, composed, counselor, versatile, good listener, wordsmith, cordial, private, fair, frank, relatable, articulate

SHADOW: the other woman, bitter, mouthy, a divorced woman, catty, brash, pushes buttons, conniving, critical, annoys easily, judge and jury, cranky, meddlesome, not easily impressed, manipulator, secret teller, vain, domineering, cutting tongue

Scene The Cassowary defiantly lifts her chin, meeting your eyes with an intense gaze. Analyzing you from head to toe, she looks for a weak spot as you dare disturb her solitude. Dismissing you as nothing to be concerned with, she jerks her head sharply, catching the moonlight on the points of her razor-sharp crown, which encircles her glorious helmet and protects her crown jewel. A Queen and victim no more, the Cassowary belongs to no one but herself, unafraid and underwhelmed, with no obligation to dole out niceties by humoring anything deemed inferior.

She's fought hard for her peace and picked up all her jagged little pieces, becoming whole once again. Always drawing unwanted attention with her size and brilliantly colored plumage, this beauty Queen is the love 'em and leave 'em kind. When she desires connection, it will always be on her terms. If challenged, she's known to be deadly, since she can fell a predator by flaying them with one swordlike kick, instantly annihilating any threat. Her brash call booms throughout the rainforest as a deep rumble and is heard echoing through the trees, shaking the ground in warning to all who dare to displease her. Fiercely protective of her peaceful environment and preferring solitude, the Queen of Swords will let no one come in the way of her happiness, because she found all she needs in herself. This was a hard lesson that took time to learn, and one she'll never forget.

Queen of Swords in Love As the most hated Queen, she is often portrayed as the other woman who has no boundaries, and everyone's fair game. Promiscuity through experimentation becomes her focus, wanting to feel something, anything, in hopes of melting the ice around her heart. She continues to jump from one relationship to another, making matters worse as rebounds become second nature, while she continues to search for love.

Queen of Swords in Career Being a domineering boss lady who's never at a loss for words makes her a prolific writer. She effortlessly gives constructive criticism both verbal and written. She is usually unimpressed and demanding and is very often hard to please. There are moments when you might see a glimmer of sensitivity, but often these are short lived, as the scowl returns, holding tension in her jaw.

Queen of Swords in Wellness Carrying a deep hurt that's festered over time leaves this Queen bitter, pushing people away. Seemingly approachable, she hides her depth well, allowing only for surface interactions. Medically, special consideration should be given in regard to acid reflux, kidneys, lower back, and ulcers.

Queen of Swords in Finances Money through divorce proceedings is a typical resource of the Queen of Swords. She's the type that would choose a financially satisfying relationship over a love connection any day. Always concerned with finances, she knows what's in her pocketbook and is keen on keeping a good account.

The Astrological Sign of the Queen of Swords Libra (September 23–October 22)

Words of Wisdom from the Queen of Swords In the shadows of my blade, I reign with relentless strength; no mercy, no compromise. I am the embodiment of judgment, wielding truth as my weapon. I am the Queen of darkness, a tempest of justice and unrest.

Spirit Guide—Cassowary She rumbles into your life as a reminder to protect the hard-earned peace you have cultivated. Trust your powerful sense of judgment when considering whom to let into your life. Let others underestimate you if they wish, for there is nothing to prove anymore. Sharpen your formidable daggerlike claws and let them try their best to disrupt your serenity, for it won't end well.

> *A really strong woman accepts the wars*
> *she went through and is ennobled by her scars.*
> **Carly Simon**

King of Swords

*With piercing eyes and a mind
sharp and keen
The King of Swords reigns,
his intellect supreme
He cuts through deceit with a
discerning blade
In wisdom and justice,
his kingdom is laid*

KEYWORDS & CONCEPTS

LIGHT: open-minded, abstract thinker, linguistic, reasonable, humanitarian, naturally talented, expressive, innovative, unique, lighthearted nature, educated, future focused, friendly, appreciative, loves to laugh, progressive, critical thinker, decisive, appropriate

SHADOW: self-absorbed, eccentric, spiteful, paradoxical, emotionally detached, loner, explosive anger, impersonal, robotic, unemotional, disagreeable, dislikes feeling tied down, unapologetic, vengeful, potty mouth, complicated, unforgiving

Scene At early dawn the Eagle pensively sits on his throne, his eagle eye fixed toward the horizon, waiting for sunrise. He ponders the source of the light as the golden rays continue cresting over the edges of the lea, touching the tips of the trees, gently awaking the world below. The sunshine gradually reaches the King, caressing his downy head and warming his silver crown as he weighs the pros and cons of flying high enough to touch the sun. With

his decision, morning officially arrives, so he spreads his expansive wings and takes off, determined to touch the sun. Higher and higher he circles, closer toward the radiant heat, approaching the source of glory. Waves of intense heat inflame his body, and a prickling sensation alerts him to danger spreading across the back of his neck, but the King pays no heed. Turning his attention inward to his mind's thoughts, he boldly states to the wind, "As sovereign to all flying creatures, I will always prevail."

His motto gives him the needed push as he courageously rises even higher, getting a better view of the light source. Freeborn, feeling the rush of wind, he's met with waves of excruciating heat. He reaches out, touching the fiery ball. Suddenly a searing pain spreads through his arm where the fire's mouth grabbed at him, singeing the tip and blackening his wing. Free-falling and barrel-rolling through the sky, riding the currents of air, he careens rapidly toward the earth. Curiously, his last conscious thought is "I will never remain earthbound. I am of air. Look to the skies, my love, for I will appear once again, rising from the wisp of smoke from my smoldering ashes." A peaceful cloak of darkness envelops his body, cradling him in a warm embrace as he feels a great sensation of being lifting upward toward the heavens. The gods gently set the Eagle back on his throne, for he is one of them—a King, Ruler of the Realm of Air. The Eagle opens his eyes and is surrounded by moonlight. A faint smell of smoke clings to the night air as he shivers, recalling the vivid dream of trying to touch the sun.

King of Swords in Love In matters of the heart, this King is as tight-lipped as they come, concealing his true feelings. His preferred mode of communication is through text, allowing him to remain impersonal and maintain control. But beneath his cold exterior lies a key to this King's heart, and it comes in the form of laughter. Laughter holds this lighthearted King's attention and is the greatest charm of his paradoxical behavior.

King of Swords in Career Naturally talented, this King is an abstract thinker, a great asset to any team. As a leader he's decisive and forward-thinking, with grand visions of the future.

King of Swords in Wellness A peculiar wellness practice for the King of Swords is a moving-sword meditation. With fluid movements and focused mindfulness, he cultivates mental clarity and inner strength, harnessing the power of the blade for physical and spiritual growth.

King of Swords in Finances Prudent when it comes to money, he is reluctant to spend and would rather make do with what he has. The truth is that the King of Swords would rather not spend any money at all, and when it comes to big purchases, he won't be the one making the suggestions.

The Astrological Sign of the King of Swords Aquarius (January 20–February 19)

Words of Wisdom from the King of Swords Why fly, when you can soar!

Spirit Guide—Bald Eagle The Eagle swoops into your life, bringing the gift of seeing things from a higher perspective. He's the bridge between you and the spiritual realms, teaching you to use the gift of sight through the art of clairvoyance. His sharp, curved talons remind mankind that his only predator is himself; being a bird of prey, he has no natural enemies. He is King.

> *But man is not made for defeat.*
> *A man can be destroyed but not defeated.*
> **Ernest Hemingway**

Ace of Pentacles

*Behold the unassuming acorn,
a World within its core
A vessel of hidden magick that many choose to ignore
Believe in manifestation, where dreams are sown as seeds
From one mighty acorn, a forest of oaks fulfill your needs*

KEYWORDS & CONCEPTS

LIGHT: new money, abundance, potential, job opportunity, new business venture, validation, seed, manifestation, financial gain, security, grounded, gifts, rewards, investments, earth element, accomplishments, new opportunity, wealth, material things, prosperity, growth

SHADOW: lack of resources, materialism, at a disadvantage, financial insecurity, missed opportunity, greed, ungrounded, scarcity, invalidated, business stagnation, gifts with strings attached, shortfall

Scene A tiny acorn house is nestled in a clearing, sitting within a ring of enchantment and emitting an eerie glow of magick. Just beyond the house lies a hidden footpath, a place to observe the house from a safe distance, since no one is ever brave enough to breach the inner sanctum. The scent of a fresh red coat of paint on the door stands out as a visual warning; this little detail is not lost on you. The sound of your own blood rushing in your ears echoes the sound of a distant stream, the closer you get to the door. Resting

by the entrance is a golden pentacle that's been there for ages, according to the local folklore you recite by rote: "Who's ever brave enough to touch the Ace of Pentacles will be blessed with copious amounts of money and showered with gifts of abundance."

The curious thing about this place is you have no idea who lives here. Rumor has it that no one's ever seen coming or going. A soft glow of candlelight can be seen through the lead windows on the second level, plunging the rest of the rooms below into darkness. You tilt your chin up, looking at the highest point of the acorn, seeing the familiar magickal lantern whose flame dances day and night, a beacon for wayward souls to find their way home. At times you wonder if you too are one of those lost souls, for life's been tough. It's been rumored that under the cover of darkness, silhouettes of figures have been seen dancing around the house, to the sound of a primitive drum that's heard beating into the night. Taking a breath, and a tentative step, then breaking out into a full out run toward the Ace of Pentacle, because you too are deserving.

Ace of Pentacles in Love Brings the best of everything to love, such as abundance, stability, connection, and deeper commitment. There might be a surprise of a proposal with the Ace of Pentacles, symbolic of a golden ring. Heralding the start of a new relationship, where respect and appreciation lay the foundation for lasting happiness.

Ace of Pentacles in Career The Ace of Pentacles brings career success with opportunities for promotions, raises, bonuses, and commissions—all these are the manifestations of this card. It signifies new business ventures and the fruitful results of your dedicated efforts, whether in a job or as an entrepreneur. Opportunities abound when this Ace is around.

Ace of Pentacles in Wellness The Ace of Pentacles brings a period of improved physical well-being and vitality, offering abundance and stability to your health journey.

Ace of Pentacles in Finances Money is on the way! Viewed as the "money card," this is a very positive sign. Signifies a financial breakthrough, bringing prosperity, wealth, and new opportunities for financial gain.

The Magick of the Ace of Pentacles Harness the enchanting power of the Ace of Pentacles. Close your eyes and vividly imagine your financial dreams coming true. As you hold an Acorn, affirm, "I effortlessly attract abundant wealth and prosperity." Take the charged Acorn and plant it, with intentions for financial success. Water it with positivity as you nourish your goals. Embrace the magick and manifest a prosperous future.

Words of Wisdom from the Ace of Pentacles Work hard but play harder. The time has come to enjoy the fruits of your labors.

Spirit of The Acorn This enchanting little nut holds the potential of a mighty forest, attracting good fortune to those who embrace its magick. Steeped in folklore, the Acorn carries a profound connection to witchcraft. It was once used as a symbol among witches, a sign of recognition and unity. Just like the mighty oak from which it comes, it is capable of living thousands of years. Carry a naturally found Acorn with you and let its gift of endurance guide and protect you on your journey.

> *Within a tiny acorn, a mighty oak is waiting!*
> *Great things always start small, so embrace beginnings*
> *and take joy in the journey.*
> **PEARL SANBORN**

Two of Pentacles

*Two coins I juggle and balance,
ticktock, the timing's right
I won't ever need to chase you,
nor do I have to use my might
Once I have my way with you, most
often you'll wind up dead
You thought it a game we're
playing, until I ripped off
your head*

KEYWORDS & CONCEPTS

LIGHT: adaptable, mobility, juggling responsibilities, reorganizing, balancing, mutable, activity, fluctuating, juggling, coordination, flow, flexible, changeable, playful, momentum, reshuffling, heads, multitasking, timing

SHADOW: variable, unstable, unfocused, uneven, flustered, out of whack, uncoordinated, shifting, unpredictable, unsettled, imbalance, uncertain, erratic, trying to juggle two things at once, in flux, tails, financial stability, overcommitment

Scene The Praying Mantis, an expert of timing, knows precisely when to lift one pentacle and lower the other. He's proud of the level of dexterity and poise he possesses, since he can manipulate the Two of Pentacles in a way that most cannot. He looks into the crowd, seeing all the frozen faces watching him intently, since half are hoping he'll fumble and fall into the frigid water, while the other half hold their breath, silently cheering him on. On cue, he slowly begins rocking back and forth, until the swing is in full motion, showing off his prowess by adding an additional element to the act. The

crowd, appreciating the degree of difficulty, explodes in a thunderous applause as the Praying Mantis eats it up.

The lights on the marquee catch his eye, *True Infinite Magick in Motion*; that's what he's determined to give them—a spectacular show, since he has mastered the art of balance. On their feet now in a feverish pitch, the crowd shouts "Encore! Encore!" The vibration of sound causes tiny little ripples in the water, making the paper boat dance and bow with enthusiasm. The Praying Mantis redoubles his efforts, sending the swing sailing into the air even higher and faster. The crowd goes wild, and right before the climax, the heavy, green, velvety curtains are drawn closed, muting the roar of the masses. Behind the scenes the Pray Mantis focuses on slowing down the swing, trying not to lose the momentum of the pentacles. He is literally stuck in the swing of things, finding it difficult to stop the movement. Now, ego aside, it becomes glaringly obvious to him that next he must learn the art of letting go.

Two of Pentacles in Love In matters of love, the Two of Pentacles represents the tumultuous nature of the relationships, where highs and lows prevail. Striving to find balance amid opposing forces is a daunting task. This card can also indicate two-timing in a relationship, juggling two people at once. For singles, managing both their dating life and home responsibilities poses a considerable challenge.

Two of Pentacles in Career Focus is on work-life balance. Both must coexist in a healthful manner. When there is imbalance in one, the other will suffer greatly. Money is important for well-being, but so is experiencing life. The Two of Pentacles appears when trying to handle multiple responsibilities and tasks simultaneously.

Two of Pentacles in Wellness Taking on too many responsibilities at once, fearing that if you let go of anything, everything will come crashing down. If you keep trying to do everything yourself, eventually you will experience a bitterness that will fester on the inside while you burn out on the outside.

Two of Pentacles in Finances Juggling your finances in order to pay your debts, by borrowing from one credit product to pay another, brings you into precarious territory. Take an accurate account of all your assets and debts and come up with realistic goals to achieve balance by actively managing your finances.

The Magick of the Two of Pentacles The Two of Pentacles unveils the power of perfect timing. Master the skill by tuning into your emotions, maintaining control, and adopting an objective perspective. Repeat the affirmation "I am cool, calm, and collected" to welcome the art of right timing.

Words of Wisdom from the Two of Pentacles Embrace the dance of life's ebb and flow, finding harmony amid chaos. Balance is key, for in the untethered moment you find grace. Trust the rhythm of time, and the right path will unfold when you are ready.

Spirit Guide—Praying Mantis In the realm of cosmic ballet, the Praying Mantis takes center stage as a maestro of timing and precision. With unwavering patience, he silently awaits the perfect moment to seize opportunity. The Mantis teaches you the art of effortless action, where you trust the divine flow and allow life's blessings to come to you. Embrace the dance of balanced abundance, orchestrating a symphony of synchronicity with each calculated move.

For him, life was a coin that had disaster
on one side and waiting for disaster on the other.
J. R. Ward

Three of Pentacles

*Together we shall build our life
as a grand design
A vow whispered to my soul,
forever yours and mine
With tireless dedication,
we pursue our shared dream
But on the other side, true
abundance is yet unseen*

KEYWORDS & CONCEPTS

LIGHT: collaboration, teamwork, apprentice, construction, work-in-progress, attempt, working, perfectionist, physical effort, crafting, student, practical use, studying, working on it, training, initiation, time-consuming

SHADOW: burning the midnight oil, uncooperative, impractical, unproductive, unappreciated, miscommunication, frustration, mediocrity, incompetence, ego clashes, undeveloped, lack of progress, disorganized, engrossed, overcompensating, nitpicking

Scene On a stony platform covered with soft green grass, the Ants are hard at work. Apprenticeship is never easy, but the job must get done, so onward they push, stacking, adjusting, and adorning the Three of Pentacles. The soft glow of the lantern's light illuminates the space, enabling the Ants to work well into the night, burning the midnight oil. Delicate daisies tremble in the wind, waiting to be plucked and wondering which one of them is next, and ponder why they have to be uprooted in order to provide beauty for something else. There is no relenting for the Ants when tasked with a job: to perfectly place all the daises on the pentacles before morning light.

Suddenly the Blue Ant notices that the job is slowing down. He feels as though it's been dragging for the last couple of hours, since not much progress is made. He looks around, seeing that the Purple Ant is not working. He is stunned, for they are the embodiment of teamwork, working collectively to reach a common goal, a prime directive of their species. He yells, "Hey, Purple Ant! Do I have to remind you that you're an Ant?" All Ants look toward the Purple, who immediately gets his act together, redoubling his efforts and contributing to the team, getting the job done ahead of schedule.

The next morning during your morning ramble, you come across a beautiful daisy-covered Three of Pentacles that greets you in the sunshine. A smile spreads across your face, for this was exactly what you needed to see to lighten the load, because lately you've become so preoccupied with work. This immediately changes your mood, as you silently thank whoever thought to create such a beautiful display.

Three of Pentacles in Love Manifests a love crafted with precision and passion. As collaborative architects, you construct a relationship masterpiece, blending your unique talents and dreams into a beautiful symphony of love and devotion. Together, you create a love story that withstands the test of time.

Three of Pentacles in Career Orchestrates the synergy of collaboration in your career. With influential partners, you will craft greatness. It's the dance of teamwork, where talent, expertise, and influence converge. Success follows your dedication to the shared vision. Together, you build a masterpiece.

Three of Pentacles in Wellness Overcoming chronic pain through collaborative efforts with healthcare professionals, physical therapists, and supportive peers, one can restore a life free from the limitations of pain.

Three of Pentacles in Finances Indicates financial rewards through collaborative efforts and skilled work. It represents recognition, advancement, influence, and wealth received through effort.

The Magick of the Three of Pentacles Experience the power of creation and fertility. Harness the energy of this card with a simple spell: light a green candle, visualize your desire manifesting, and affirm that "I am fertile, abundant, and joyful in bringing forth my desires."

Words of Wisdom from the Three of Pentacles Collectively, Clotho, Lachesis, and Atropos, the Three Fates, intricately weave life's tapestry, infusing the Three of Pentacles with timeless magick and abundant destinies.

Spirit Guide—Ant The industrious Ant crawls into your life, bringing the gift of teamwork. Through perseverance, the Ant tirelessly works together with its colony, building intricate tunnels and gathering provisions. It teaches you the value of cooperation through shared goals. Trust in you ability to contribute to the greater good and achieve success through collective effort. The Ant's unwavering determination and work ethic will guide you on a path of success, reminding you that even the smallest steps can lead to great achievements. Embrace the spirit of unity and diligence as you navigate life.

> *There is nothing impossible to him who will try.*
> **Alexander the Great**

Four of Pentacles

*Guarding my treasures,
holding them close, never to share
Afraid to lose what I possess,
clutching with utmost care
In secrets I find solace, but my
heart yearns for release
If only I will let go, then abundance
can bring me peace*

KEYWORDS & CONCEPTS

LIGHT: stability, security, material wealth, possessiveness, saving, prudence, acquisitions, hold on, frugal, centered, preparedness, resources, keeping things close to the chest, personal space, financial control, conservation

SHADOW: secrets, greedy, miser, apprehensive, hoarding, insecurity, strangling, attachments, selfish, terrified of material loss, scarcity mindset, penniless, blocked potential

Scene The Squirrel tightly clutches the golden pentacle to her chest. She's dealt with swindlers and thieves before and won't take the chance of losing everything again. Tucked away in her hidey-hole, she feels the protection of the cool earthen burrow, as the dragonflies stir above, watching for intruders. Turning her attention back to her biggest prize yet, the coveted Four of Pentacles, she turns it, admiring its weight and shine reflected back, gold gleaming in her eyes. The dragonflies swiftly descend into the burrow in a tizzy, whizzing and frantically moving in a flurry of warning. Her eyebrows knit together as she looks around earnestly to see what the commotion is all about. Her eyes widen a bit before stiffening and freezing in place, with nary a blink, breath, or twitch of her whiskers. Her eyes connect with an eyeball looking into her burrow.

Your presence alone creates panic, as she's overcome by an uncomfortable wave of heat. Instinctively clutching the pentacle tighter, a prickle of uncertainty settles over as she feels that her secrets might be discovered. A bead of sweat slowly rolls down her brow, dripping into her eye. Not budging, she stares at the eyeball watching her. What seems like eternity, realizing she can't keep this charade up much longer, she tentatively blinks once and waits, and nothing happens. She blinks again, narrowing her eyes, yet no reaction from the intruder. A smile slips from her lips, content that her secrets are safe. She continues squirreling away her treasures. Convincing herself you're just a figment of her imagination, she suddenly freezes again as she hears a voice say, "Nah, there's nothing in there, just a squirrel."

Four of Pentacles in Love In matters of love, the Four of Pentacles suggests the presence of a hidden secret. It signifies a selfish dynamic with a relationship, with one partner prioritizing their needs over the other's. If single, be wary of ambiguous intentions from potential suitors. Transparency and open communication are key for healthful relationships.

Four of Pentacles in Career In the workplace, the Four of Pentacles reveals a firm grip on resources, fostering an atmosphere of possessiveness and secrecy. Strive for openness and collaboration, for true success lies in fostering a work environment of trust and shared knowledge. Let go to gain abundance.

Four of Pentacles in Wellness Reveals the price of holding on to secrets; they fester, zapping the freedom of fully living. This poison buried deep within manifests as physical ailments and imbalances. Come clean and release anything weighing on your conscience; if not, suffer the detrimental consequences to well-being.

Four of Pentacles in Finances Squirreling away funds for a rainy day symbolizes a strong emphasis on savings, budgeting, and financial stability. It warns of miserly holding on to your purse strings, placing immense importance on material possessions, and obsessing over accumulating wealth.

The Magick of the Four of Pentacles Releasing attachments: When the Moon is waning, stand under her radiant light and visualize the thing that holds your attention. Let the Moon's energy intertwine with your emotions and swirl around, encompassing your attachment. With each intentional breath, release the grip of the enchantment, letting go of the energy that no longer serves you. As the Moon embraces your offering, feel the weight lift from your spirit, making room for new blessing to delight your life.

Words of Wisdom from the Four of Pentacles Secrets are a double-edged sword. They can protect or destroy lives.

Spirit Guide—Squirrel As the lively Squirrel scampers into your world, it brings a powerful message of balance between material wealth and inner fulfillment. Just like the Squirrel collects and stores acorns, you may find yourself accumulating possessions. But remember, true happiness lies not in the abundance of things, but in the richness of experiences and connections. The Squirrel reminds you to simplify your life. Don't be a hoarder. Instead, embrace the joy and freedom that comes from less.

*Humanity appreciates truth about as much
as a squirrel appreciates silver.*
Vernon Howard

Five of Pentacles

*In the struggle to survive,
I'll do whatever it takes
Willing to do anything, and yes,
I've made mistakes
Things that I'm not proud of,
things I'll never say
Done with the sole purpose of just
to live another day*

KEYWORDS & CONCEPTS

LIGHT: hardship, financial woes, perseverance, resilience, asking for help, settling, lessons learned, worried, concern, asking for handouts, struggles, scarcity, abstain, misfortune, enduring, isolated, limitations

SHADOW: desperation, poverty, lack of support, poor health, left out, hardship, begging, financial ruin, outcast, destitute, shunned, stress and anxiety, lacking necessities, false promises, imposed limitations

Scene The clever Opossum positions herself right at the sight line of the door, to gain sympathy from the people passing by while begging for handouts. Downtrodden and destitute, she's been through many hardships and seen the ugliness of life. She's made a comfy home in the mossy-colored high-backed chair, perfectly positioned in line with the key's access point. The problem is, no one has come by for some time. Lately, people are numbingly content to wander around blindly, ignoring her plight and the door of consciousness. She's been waiting for any enlightened soul to walk through

the door, so she too can slip through, giving her youngsters a better life. She cocks her head, and a sound suddenly prick her ears. Immediately stiffening, she plays dead.

After searching for hours, you finally find the illusive door with the Five of Pentacles. Strange, since you've been down this road a thousand times but never saw the door. Looking around, you see the keys conveniently hanging by the lantern, its glow beckoning you closer. Taking a sidelong glance at the ratty old chair, you keep a safe distance while assessing the situation. Biting the inside of your cheek, your gaze rests on the sickly-looking animal, recoiling as you see hideous furry things moving around, "Babies!" Making no sudden movements, you feel the adrenaline pumping as you gingerly reach over to grasp the keys. The slight jangle causes you to freeze and hold your breath, as you can smell the stench of death permeating the air. Looking back at the momma now, you are sure she's dead. All tension leaves your body as you turn, facing the door, and insert the key. You wait to hear a click as you push down on the latch, swinging the door wide open, and you walk through. Suddenly you feel something brush against your leg; your stomach flutters, making your skin crawl. As you look down and see a shadow scurry away, you shudder as you look back and see an empty chair.

Five of Pentacles in Love In a relationship, this card signifies profound hardships and broken promises, causing a constant state of anxious neediness. The fear of abandonment and feeling neglected weighs heavily, draining the relationship of warmth and hope. It's a reminder that love shouldn't feel so cold and desolate. Reevaluate your relationship and ask yourself, "Is it worth it?"

Five of Pentacles in Career In the bleak realm of career, the Five of Pentacles reveals a stark portrait of rejection and financial hardship. It casts a shadow of being overlooked and unappreciated in the workplace, evoking even more disgruntled feelings of being passed up and not earning enough.

Five of Pentacles in Wellness The Five of Pentacles casts a shadow on health and wellness, manifesting as physical and emotional afflictions. It reflects a state of shambles, where health suffers amid financial struggles.

After prolonged periods, emotional afflictions may be presented as bouts of stress and anxiety. Use breath exercises and journaling to get you through prickly moments.

Five of Pentacles in Finances Scarcity, struggling to make ends meet, facing mounting debts, and limited resources bring about desperation and fear. Accept your situation and change it. Borrow or beg; receive handouts, donations, or anything to help get you on your feet.

The Magick of the Five of Pentacles The magick of the Five of Pentacles is mutable; its power lies in its essence, shaped by the interplay of surrounding cards. Welcome the transformative power by wielding intention and spells to transcend limitations. Embrace the boundless potential that lies within this redefining moment. Nothing is impossible!

Words of Wisdom from the Five of Pentacles From winter's shadow of despair, emerge like a fragile blossom, resilient and blooming in the face of adversity.

Spirit Guide—Opossum As one of the most accomplished actors, the Opossum emerges as your guide. In the realm of make-believe, this master of transformation teaches you the art of adapting to challenging circumstances. As you navigate through the darkest moments, embrace your resilience and wear the mask of endurance. With keen perception, see beyond illusions and uncover hidden truths. Explore the depths of power to rise above any struggle, and transform hardship into triumph.

Remember, the Opossum has the ability to "play dead" so convincingly that the stench of death physically lingers in the air, allowing it to live another day.

Man never made any material as resilient as the human spirit.
Bernard Williams

Six of Pentacles

With open heart and hands,
I share my wealth and gain
A giver and receiver,
in harmony we remain
Balancing scales of giving,
each act a seed is sown
Abundance flows freely,
compassion brightly shown

KEYWORDS & CONCEPTS

LIGHT: generosity, fairness, charity, give and take, support, financial assistance, equal exchange, generosity, gratitude, mercy, sharing, decency, bartering, distribution, philanthropy, compassion, delicate balance, giving handouts, procuring

SHADOW: stipulations, strings attached, expenditures, gluttony, squandering, extortion, arrears, overdue payments, freeloading, unreliable, selfishness, unfair, stinginess, misuse of power, financial losses, manipulation, unreciprocated

Scene On a fine summer's day, the Labrador Retriever stands in front of a circular door in the midst of a dense wooded area. Soulful intelligent eyes connect with yours, silently offering to share her Six of Pentacles. You're overcome with an intense desire to reach out and touch the top of that silky head, but for now you're content to watch the scene unfold at a distance. The Fox keeps licking her lips with anticipation as the badger rocks back and forth, fixated on the basket of goodies. Curiously, you keep watching as the

Labrador Retriever continues standing sentinel at her post, not budging, as if frozen in place. Suddenly the sneaky fox lets out a shrill laugh as she slyly nips the Labrador on the ankle. The retriever is startled by the attack, and the basket of pentacles is upset, tumbling and raining down money as the dog yelps and takes off running. You gasp, keeping your head down, but still intently watching as the badger collects the pentacles, depositing them on the door's threshold as an offering.

Your eyes slowly widen, not believing the scene before you. You lean in for a proper look, and the round door starts whirling and twirling; the fox and the badger were there one moment and gone the next. As you touch the back of your hand to your forehead, trying to make sense of what just happened, the Labrador comes racing back, leaping into the shimmering center and disappearing as well. Tipping your head back and letting out a robust laugh, you shout, "The door is a portal, and magick is real!" You've seen it happen right before your eyes. Quiet now, you turn your head, having a good look around, and see nothing special. Everything looks exactly the same as it does every day when you walk in the woods.

Six of Pentacles in Love In the art of the sacred balance of giving and receiving, where hearts intertwine in an equal exchange, embrace the power of generosity. Cultivate a love that flows abundantly in both directions, creating a reciprocal, blissful connection.

Six of Pentacles in Career Sometimes you have to give a little to further your position in your career. Stay a bit later, do a bit more, have skin in the game, and care about your job by having pride in your work. You'll be greatly rewarded when you approach work this way, versus doing the bare minimum to earn a paycheck.

Six of Pentacles in Wellness The ancient wisdom of the Six of Pentacles reveals the power of giving and receiving. By understanding the interconnectedness of energy flow, you unlock the hidden potential for healing.

Six of Pentacles in Finances Illuminates the eternal Law of Balance in finances, since the scales always find equilibrium, ensuring that what we give aligns with what we receive. The energy we put forth will be returned to us in unexpected ways, for the universe abhors voids. Embrace the cosmic dance of reciprocity, being mindful of your actions.

The Magick of the Six of Pentacles Remember that giving to others rewards you in ways you never thought possible. This is the magick of the Six of Pentacles: the more you give, the more you get.

Words of Wisdom from the Six of Pentacles You will leave this life with what you came with. When you understand this, you be afforded the freedom to savor all life's moments untethered.

Spirit Guide—Labrador Retriever In a world where kindness is the currency of the soul, the Labrador Retriever bounds into your life with the gift of compassion. Its warm gaze and gentle touch resonate deep within, stirring a thread of empathy that pulls at your heart. With each wag of her tail, she rouses emotions of love and connection, reminding you of the power of selfless giving. As you welcome the Labrador's beautiful spirit, let your heart expand with generosity, knowing that your acts of kindness create ripples of joy and transform lives.

No act of kindness, no matter how small, is ever wasted.
Aesop

Seven of Pentacles

I plant you in the soil,
with hopes that you'll grow
Nursing each moment,
as nature's secrets I sow
Waiting for the harvest, when
abundance comes alive
In patient anticipation,
success will soon arrive

KEYWORDS & CONCEPTS

LIGHT: patience, harvest, growing, reflection, productive, rewards, investment, appraisal, progress, long game, cultivation, potential, waiting, delayed gratification, hard work pays off, fruition, reevaluation, anticipation, development, reaping what you sow, right time

SHADOW: hate and wait, impatience, doubt, stagnation, unproductive, frustration, antsy, futile, discouraged, performance anxiety, setbacks, unsuccessful, stalling, inattentive, neglected, failure, money pit

Scene One foggy night, the magician's Rabbit did his own disappearing act, right into the thickets of the woods, with only the glow of a lantern lighting his way through the darkness. Every opportunity to sneak out is worth it, as he races to check on the progress of his tree project. All these years he's learned a magick trick of his own; once you plant a fertile seed, something will grow. Setting his wheelbarrow aside, standing before a gnarled limb laden with Seven of Pentacles, he whispers lovingly, "Soon." That same

night, the magician thought something was terribly amiss when he couldn't find his hat, aside from that he's caught on to the nightly disappearance of his faithful act. During intermission the magician followed him out. When the Rabbit turned to set down the wheelbarrow, the magician quickly darted out, crouching into the shadow of the hideous tree.

The glow of moonlight hung in the night's crisp air, highlighting a few pentacles ripe for the picking. Looking onto his flourishing tree, the Rabbit felt a rush of pride; all his hard work will soon pay off, and he'll have enough money to leave. Donning the magick hat between his ears, the Rabbit goes into planning mode, creating a mental tally of "what ifs." He freezes because something feels off, chewing the inside of his cheek, waiting for the panic to subside. Minutes pass as the Rabbit stretches toward the ripest pentacle, pausing in midair, and then slowly lowers his paws. He just can't shake the feeling that something is off. Suddenly the magician springs from behind the tree, startling the Rabbit into a backward stumble. Seizing an opportunity, the magician lunges out with deft fingers, and a "hocus-pocus" later he pushes down the magickal hat, then swoops the Rabbit up inside, saying, "Gotcha!" One moment the Rabbit remembers reaching for a pentacle, and the next he is encased in darkness, sighing, "I'm back in the hat." No tears came because he knows: it was in the same darkness he planted a wee seed, and it was under the darkness of fertile earth that tiny seed grew, and so did he.

Seven of Pentacles in Love A card of waiting and patience, the Seven of Pentacles reminds you to trust the timing of love. Sometimes we must cultivate and nurture the relationship, allowing it to bloom in its own time. True love requires tending and patience.

Seven of Pentacles in Career Cultivate patience in your career path. Resist the allure of pursuing promotions and collecting titles. Accept divine timing, for the right people will notice your talents. Let progress unfold naturally, witnessing the magnificent blossoming of your success.

Seven of Pentacles in Wellness Uncover the secret garden within, where seeds of vitality lie dormant. Foster patience as you tend to your well-being, for beneath the surface a fruitful field awaits. Nourish the roots of self-care and watch as vibrant blooms of health and vitality unfold in the most-unexpected ways.

Seven of Pentacles in Finances Plant the seeds of financial abundance with patience and perseverance. Your efforts may not yield immediate results, but trust in the process. Nurture your resources, make wise investments, and watch as your financial garden blooms.

The Magick of the Seven of Pentacles The Seven of Pentacles holds the enchantment of transmutation. To harness this power, take seeds of wildflowers and scatter them into the wind, visualizing your desires multiplying and blooming in the world. Watch as the universe answers, bringing forth the harvest of your intentions.

Words of Wisdom from the Seven of Pentacles Patience tends the soil of dreams, allowing them to blossom in their own time. Greatness emerges from the warm embrace of acceptance.

Spirit Guide—Rabbit As the Rabbit hops into your life, he brings whispers of fertility and the promise of fruition. With intention and focus, keep your goals at the forefront of your mind. Like seeds of wildflowers dancing in the wind, seize the opportunities presented to you. Always seek the advantage of perfect timing. Find the path that leads to success, for it awaits your gentle touch.

I'm late, I'm late! For a very important date!
No time to say, "hello, goodbye," I'm late, I'm late, I'm late!
White Rabbit, *Alice in Wonderland*

Eight of Pentacles

*With unwavering focus,
hone my craft, nose to the grind
Every stroke and every detail,
part of a masterful design
A symphony of skills, a conducted
virtuoso at my work
My passion fuels the art;
working then becomes a perk*

KEYWORDS & CONCEPTS

LIGHT: dedication, mastery, skill, professionalism, arrangements, focus on career, productivity, inventory, meticulous, craftsmanship, diligence, pride in work, expertise, committed, honing your craft, accomplishments, projects, practicing, order, showmanship

SHADOW: monotony, overworked, repetition, complacent, tediousness, workaholism, inefficiency, tunnel vision, uncreative, unrealistic expectations, exhaustion, unrewarding work, unprofessional, laborious, demolish, engrossed, lazy, wasteful (resources)

Scene Three Rats are hard at work, tasked with repairing the Eight of Pentacles on the front of the tiny house. They were hired on as master craftsmen because only perfection will do. Being the best in the business, there's no room for sloppiness or a rushed job, since their reputation is always at stake, so they continue working well into the evening. As the final touches are being made, Mr. Browne can't quite get the last pentacle up. He's fussing

and fidgeting but can't seem to get the last one to stick. Mr. Red looks up intently, giving directions as best as he can. This low light is really making it hard to see. Now pushing well past quitting time, the job is dragging. The ingenious Mr. Red instantly solves this issue by catching a firefly, securing it in the cage and flooding the space with better lighting.

Watching this display, Mr. Black rolls his eyes, thinking, "Of course, the boss has *all* the answers!" How's he always "the ladder guy"; the only task ever assigned to him was "Black! Hold steady and support Mr. Browne." Disgruntled and feeling undervalued, Mr. Black pouts and sulks, upset about being given such a menial task. He mutters, "It should've been me up there. And if it were me, we'd be home by now." Beyond irritated, Mr. Black yells up at Mr. Browne, "Stop being such a perfectionist! Let's go!" The other Rats ignore the outburst, causing Mr. Black's mood to darken as a caustic energy permeates the air, aggravating Mr. Browne further as he fumbles once again. Mr. Red has had enough, turning to Mr. Black and snapping, "Cool it!" Now, Mr. Black's mood turns as black as his name. Having none of this, he inconspicuously lays a hand gently across the most rickety part of the ladder, tempted to give it a little shove. Slowly he starts applying the tiniest bit of pressure when he hears Mr. Browne say, "Got it!" Mr. Red frees the firefly; lights out, as another day is done.

Eight of Pentacles in Love Signifies dedication. Investing the time and effort into building a solid foundation, honing your skills as a generous partner, and continuously striving for improvement will create a lasting and fulfilling soulful connection.

Eight of Pentacles in Career As the work card, the Eight of Pentacles brings hard work, focus, and mastery of your craft. Indicates a dedicated pursuit of excellence and a commitment to continual learning and improvement, with the potential for acknowledgments as one of the "greats" in your chosen profession.

Eight of Pentacles in Wellness Beware of workaholic tendencies. Seek balance with small, mindful movements to quell the busy mind, thus channeling your energy into a more healthful direction.

Eight of Pentacles in Finances Master your craft, tirelessly striving for excellence. Ascend to financial abundance and coveted status through unwavering dedication. The Eight of Pentacles empowers your relentless pursuit of success.

The Magick of the Eight of Pentacles The magickal ritual of Honing Your Craft: Gather materials representing your work or craft, such as tools or symbolic objects. Light an orange candle and focus on your intention to enhance your skills and attract abundance. As you work on honing your craft, visualize your goals manifesting. Offer gratitude to the Universe for the opportunities and progress.

Words of Wisdom from the Eight of Pentacles Master your craft with unwavering devotion. Each work shapes the masterpieces of your life's work.

Spirit Guide—Rat As the Rat scurries into your life, it brings the gift of adaptability and a tireless work ethic. These qualities ensure your survival and enable you to thrive in any environment. The Rat's highly social nature and shrewdness guarantee a lasting legacy. Immerse yourself in the art of attention to detail, for every stroke you make adds to the grand masterpiece. Take pride in your work, since it shapes your destiny.

I do not wish to comment on the work;
if it does not speak for itself, it is a failure.
George Orwell

Nine of Pentacles

*Pretty high-born paramour
desires a life of luxury
Wearing expensive brands,
for all the world to see
Enjoying an opulent lifestyle,
paid by someone else
Living her best life,
always thinking about herself*

KEYWORDS & CONCEPTS

LIGHT: affluence, abundance, financial independence, gratitude, luxury, life's easy, cultured, material comforts, bountiful, a garden, opulence, styled, cornucopia, birthright, financial security, couture, lifestyle, enjoyment, polished, lavish

SHADOW: dependency, materialism, pretentious, envious, manipulative, spoiled, nonchalant, jealousy, inconsiderate, bribable, ungrateful, flaunting, vain, unappreciative, extravagant

Scene The Snail stands at the edge of the garden, admiring her new hat in the limpid aquamarine Pool of Reflection. The greens and blues of the peacock feathers play off the ripples of the mirrored surface, admiring the face looking back. She's more than comfortable staying within the boundaries of her luxurious confines, resigned to live out the rest of her days in the lap of luxury. Everyone who passes can see the stark golden luster of the Nine of

Pentacles proudly displayed above her home's door. The pride of ownership is obvious. She looks to the brass door's filigree and smiles as she traces the etching on the wooden sign with her finger, repeating the phrase "Home Sweet Home." Is it, though? She wonders.

She has everything she desires, and she should be happy, but with great abundance comes a great deal of responsibility. She learned long ago that money does not create happiness. Life didn't start off that easy for the Snail, since she had to learn this lesson the hard way. As a young Snail she chased the opulent lifestyle, ending up in a financial relationship. Everything was blissful, but as time went on, a shroud of melancholy overcame her as she became a prisoner of her own circumstance. Even though she had everything, the reality is that she really had nothing, because of the hollow of emptiness this lifestyle created. Now, every day she comes to the pool to reflect on how she ended up becoming someone's possession, trying to discover a path to independence so she can rebuild her life. But most importantly, to rebuild herself and once again feel comfortable in her skin.

Nine of Pentacles in Love Cautioning against superficial connections, this card warns of someone loving your money more than you. Seek true love that transcends the constraints of materialism.

Nine of Pentacles in Career The Nine of Pentacles warns of potential envy and jealousy from others in the workplace. Beware of those who question your achievements, or position, attributing them to favoritism rather than relying on your own merits.

Nine of Pentacles in Wellness In the shadows of the garden, the Nine of Pentacles reveals the haunting truth. The body mirrors everything your mind cannot let go; frown lines appear as laughter disappears. Changing your appearance on the outside will never change how you feel on the inside. So spend time in the garden, savoring the peace of your surroundings as you direct serenity inward.

Nine of Pentacles in Finances Signifies financial independence and abundance, having enough to appreciate the finer things in life. It represents the rewards of hard work, discipline, and wise financial decisions. Enjoy the fruits of your labor. Savor the luxury and comforts that money can buy, but just make sure that your wallet can support your lifestyle.

The Magick of the Nine of Pentacles This is an optimal time for money spells. Take a green candle, carve a pentacle, light it, and affirm that "I have a deep and unshakable belief in my ability to manifest wealth and create financial success."

Words of Wisdom from the Nine of Pentacles Be careful not to get trapped in your own prison of materialism.

Spirit Guide—Snail The gentle Snail gracefully glides into your life, reminding you to embrace the essence of self-sufficiency and abundance. Just as the Snail carries its home on its back, you possess everything you need within you. Take solace in your own company and find joy in the simple pleasures of life. Slow and steady progress leads to the fulfillment of your desires. Cultivate a sense of inner riches, for it radiates outward, attracting prosperity and contentment.

If you live off a man's compliments, you'll die from his criticism.
Cornelius Lindsey

Ten of Pentacles

In the tapestry of life,
our lineage does entwine
Generations bound together,
an ancestral design
Weaving wealth and prosperity,
a legacy so grand
Tenfold blessings bestowed,
in our familial land

KEYWORDS & CONCEPTS

LIGHT: legacy, stability, supportive family, inheritance, prosperity, lineage, well established, security, tradition, wealth, longevity, blessings, reputation, generational wealth, bloodlines, ancestry, goals realized, attainment

SHADOW: entitlement, social-status snob, inheritance disputes, excessive attachments, dysfunction, inherited burdens, family conflict, lost traditions, family money, ancestral wounds

Scene The yule tree's alit with hundreds of flickering tiny lights as the family of Elephants gathers at their special spot, among the December daisies. In the background, festive music plays and notes float up through the air, as the trees join in harmony. The little ones' eyes are aglow with the anticipation of opening up all the pretty wrapped gifts, beckoning to be ripped open so their treasures can be revealed. The spirit of the season surrounds them as familiar smells waft from the stone oven, bringing back memories of bygone eras. The palatable excitement hangs in the air, as the baby Elephants look

up at their momma, expectantly asking, "Is it time yet? Can we open our presents? *Pleeeeease?*" Momma smiles at the boys. "No, it's not time," she says, and walks slowly toward the chest containing the Ten of Pentacles. She explains the importance of gratitude by acknowledging all the abundance bestowed onto the family as another year comes to a close.

The time is nigh, so momma begins reciting the story of yule, a family tradition she's carried forward that the little ones have come to wait for, year after year. Enthralled with the tale, the littlest one curls up at momma's feet, all safe and warm, trying desperately to keep those heavy lids from closing as the sound of mamma's voice lulls him into sleep. At the stroke of midnight, big, fluffy snowflakes start softly falling in the woods, tickling their trunks and clinging to their lacy lashes. The festivities awaken the littlest one just in time. As the moon moves into midnight, he quickly joins the others, opening gifts, laughing, and eating as the family celebrates another prosperous year together, surrounded by love.

Ten of Pentacles in Love This card weaves a tapestry of love and eternal devotion, transcending time and space. Together build a sanctuary of love, where every breath is a symphony of passion and every touch ignites eternal flames.

Ten of Pentacles in Career This card signifies a period of great achievement that will be abundantly rewarded. Remember that with each tiny step you take, you are contributing to your wealth empire. If self-employed, the focus is on building a successful business and eventually succession planning.

Ten of Pentacles in Wellness Reveals a profound connection between ancestral health and personal well-being. Look to your roots for hidden wisdom and healing practices that have been passed down through generations. Honor the strength of family bonds and revere the legacy of holistic practices and herbalism that still echo in your soul.

Ten of Pentacles in Finances Spend some accumulated wealth on making memories, an invaluable family experience to be enjoyed for years to come. The focus of the Ten of Pentacles also speaks to generational wealth, leaving something behind to be enjoyed by future generations.

The Magick of the Ten of Pentacles Create an ancestral altar in your home, in honor of the ones who've come before and who have left memories and family traditions behind in your heart.

Words of Wisdom from the Ten of Pentacles Leave something behind for future generations to remember you by.

Spirit Guide—African Grey Elephant The Elephant comes trumpeting into your life; touching her trunk to you in greeting, after a quick sniff she welcomes you. This gentle giant carries the collective memory of her ancestors, reminding you of the importance of family and heritage. Embrace the values of loyalty and family, for they form the foundation of enduring wealth and abundance. Just as the African Grey Elephant moves gracefully through the land, navigate life through the societies you build around the traditions of your ancestors. Remember, true richness lies not only in material possessions, but also in the love and connection shared with your loved ones.

*Elephants will never abandon their friends or family,
but man does. I guess that's what makes us civilized.*
Anthony T. Hincks

Page of Pentacles

*Eager anticipation fuels my steps
on this path of grown-up grace
Exploring the realms of knowledge
with a youthful embrace
Seeking wisdom and skills,
eager to learn and grow
With each new endeavor, a world of
possibilities I sow*

KEYWORDS & CONCEPTS

LIGHT: perseverance, tactile, studious, musical, consistent, realist, analytical, truthful, pragmatic, conscientious, precise, intellectual, observant, team player, dedicated, cultured, brilliant, autonomous, poetic, academic

SHADOW: bullheaded, tactless, novice, serious, reactive, rationalize, possessiveness, laziness, materialistic, disobedient, procrastinator, headstrong, perfectionist, unmotivated, retaliation, poetic justice, bookworm, unrealistic

Scene A studious Piglet looks up at you, bemused, wondering what brings you this way. You slowly approach; raising your hand and smiling, you say, "I'm on a hike, just passing through." His eyes sparkle with intrigue, as he proceeds to tell you all about his love of books, grabbing the top one off the pile, his favorite one: *The Commuter Pig Keeper* by Michaela Giles. You raise your eyebrows as a loud guffaw escapes your lips, keenly observing the Piglet's sheepish smile. Decision made, you stop for a little chat, since you're dying to know what's with the hat!

Taking a seat on the lush grass, your eyes float up to get a better look at the hat, as the words come flying out of your mouth: "Why are you wearing such a large hat with a star?" The Piglet, amused that you cared to ask, straightens himself up to appear taller and says, "Oh, because I'm the Page of Pentacles." You glance around slack-mouthed, looking for a clue as to what the Piglet's talking about. When nothing comes, your lips form an awkward smile as you continue to sit in silence. The Piglet's intelligent eyes light up as he absentmindedly touches his hat and proceeds in an important voice to tell you all about the Page of Pentacles. Listening intently, appreciating such a thorough lecture, you're kind of glad you stopped to speak with this curious little creature. In a gesture of friendship, you reach into your rucksack, pulling out your favorite novel, showing the Piglet that you too enjoy a good book. You get up, brushing stray blades of grass off your knees, and hold out your parting gift. Accepting the book, the Piglet smugly reads the title, *Weird Pig* by Robert Long Foreman, crushing the treasure to his chest and letting out a squeal of happiness. You wave goodbye to your newfound friend, shaking your head and walking back to the trail, thinking how wonderfully strange the whole encounter was.

Page of Pentacles in Love The Page of Pentacles in love is drawn to beauty and physical attraction, easily captivated by the allure of their partner. Honesty is crucial to them, since they have a keen memory for past transgressions. When they fall in love, they commit deeply and may even consider marriage. However, be cautious of their possessive tendencies, for love may turn into an entangled dance.

Page of Pentacles in Career The ultimate worker bee, the Page of Pentacles thrives as a valuable team member, excelling in diverse fields that require hands-on expertise. From construction and culinary arts to engineering and music, this talented Page is committed to ensuring success and fulfillment in their chosen vocation. They are inquisitive and studious, bringing diligence and dedication to any workplace. The Page of Pentacles is always a valuable team member.

Page of Pentacles in Wellness This Page may experience throat-related issues such as throat and nasal discomfort or swollen glands. It is important for them to pay attention to their throat chakra and to express their feelings and emotions through words, promoting overall well-being and balance.

Page of Pentacles in Finances You have to work for it. Nothing comes easy for this Page. Only dedication and hard work will yield financial rewards.

The Astrological Sign of the Page of Pentacles Taurus (April 20–May 20)

Words of Wisdom from the Page of Pentacles Tend the soil of your ambition, for within lies the secret to infinite growth. With patient devotion, manifest a world where dreams materialize and you become the master of your own flourishing destiny.

Spirit Guide—Piglet With a delightful grunt and an oink, the Piglet waddles into your life, carrying the energy of growth, consistency, and dedication. Just as the Piglet eagerly explores its surroundings, allow yourself to embrace new experiences and opportunities with a sense of wonder. Learn from the Piglet's gift of diligence, saving for the future as you develop the habit of setting aside resources for your dreams and aspirations. Trust in your abilities and nurture the seeds of prosperity, for the treasure of abundance awaits your dedication. Keep putting your money in the piggy bank, for it represents your commitment to saving and seizing the next great opportunity that presents itself.

> *I am fond of pigs. Dogs look up to us.*
> *Cats look down on us. Pigs treat us as equals.*
> **Winston Churchill**

Knight of Pentacles

*Looking over the landscape,
far as the eye can see
Every step forward I take frees
a little part of me
Sometimes it's hard to leave
familiar things behind
By moving toward my future,
a brand new life I find*

KEYWORDS & CONCEPTS

LIGHT: bringer of messages, patient, communicates through touch, diligent, measured steps, ruled by material things, stable, practical, reconsidering, learns through experience, pursuit of happiness, orderly, down to earth, attention to detail, patient, casual, methodical, loves his possessions

SHADOW: not moving forward, reserved, unambitious, tight-lipped, impasse, can't see the path, overcautious, regimented, counterproductive, apprehensive, stubbornness, unsure how to proceed, resistant to change, thorough, reluctant, fastidious

Scene The Knight of Pentacles stands still in a field of daisies. A gentle breeze moves through the foggy hollow, lifting the silky strands of his silvery-gold mane. Looking into the distance, he falls deep into thought, whispering to the wind, "What's my next move?" His immediate thoughts turn to folly, as he snaps out of his daydream. He shakes his head and says aloud, "Imagine asking the wind for answers." Awake, he is afraid to move, in fear of making

the wrong maneuver and sabotaging his progress thus far. His tail swishes back and forth in rhythmic irritation; it's very unlike him being so preoccupied with his thoughts. He repeatedly paws the ground in frustration, disturbing the tender beauties under hoof, foreshadowing his trampled dreams.

Standing so unnaturally still goes against his very essence, for he was born to run. His eyes diligently scan the landscape, looking for anything that could be blocking his path. Once again he hesitates, because it's always the unseen things that get you in the end. Tendrils of steam blow out of his nose, as he neighs forcefully and defiantly into the night sky, his patience resting on thin ice. Ruled by tangible results, this Knight's dilemma is that he cannot see the end goal, which makes him feel insecure about his next steps in this uncharted territory. Just when he needs encouragement, the golden hue of the lanterns lights up the pentacle on his flank, motivating him to move toward his vision. Feeling the light gently caress the pentacle on his third eye, it reminds him that when you cannot see with your physical eyes, tap into your intuition. The light reminds the Knight of everything he needs to take the first tentative steps forward.

Knight of Pentacles in Love A beacon of unwavering dedication, this Knight traverses the realm of love with measured steps. Once he finds his person, he dons his shining armor, ready to begin a profound journey of lasting devotion, illuminating the path with steadfast commitment.

Knight of Pentacles in Career In the workplace this Knight learns through experience and, in turn, teaches others, making him the quintessential trainer or supervisor, imparting wisdom to others. With his presence, stability reigns, offering a sense of security in employment.

Knight of Pentacles in Wellness The Knight of Pentacles brings a period of stability and consistency in health matters. If inquiring about a specific situation, it suggests that there will be no significant change or fluctuations.

Knight of Pentacles in Finances With steady progress and a methodical approach to wealth, this Knight works diligently toward financial stability, ensuring no changes that could disrupt his carefully planned finances. Patience and persistence are rewarded as money gradually accumulates, providing a solid foundation.

The Movement of the Knight of Pentacles The Knight of Pentacles represents aspects associated with earth signs, As bringers of messages and the embodiment of pure energy, all Knights are depicted by horses, associated with specific movements, energy, and speed of timing. This is the slowest Knight of the deck, since he is at a standstill. When the Knight of Pentacles shows up, it predicts a time of stagnation or something happening very slowly and methodically, one step at a time. This Knight brings messages of actual events.

Words of Wisdom from the Knight of Pentacles Wisdom lies in patience, for in the realm of steady steps, greatness unfurls when readiness meets opportunity. So, I will take my time and not be rushed into anything until I'm good and ready!

Spirit Guide—Icelandic Horse The Icelandic is known for its unique gait, where one foot is always connected to the ground. As a symbol of fertility, the Icelandic is here to encourage you to take a step forward in realizing your goals while remaining grounded. Good-natured, with an unwavering confidence, this beautifully maned horse reminds you to take pride in your outward appearance. Embrace your hesitation, since it is alerting you to something, but know when to start moving again with deliberate steps and stride toward your goals. This spirit animal brings resilience, with the ability to thrive in the harshest of climates, demonstrating that no matter what you face, you'll be able to get through.

No horse can go as fast as the money you put on it.
Earl Wilson

Queen of Pentacles

*Follow me through the thickets
of life, as I will be your guide
Trust that I can see the way through;
I'll never leave your side
Many times you'll be challenged,
until the lessons are learned
The journey will not be easy,
navigating life's twists and turns*

KEYWORDS & CONCEPTS

LIGHT: practical, efficient, attentive, nurturer, organized, health conscious, calm, analytical, faithful, gracious, recollective, responsible, grateful, kind, prepared, grounded, smart, humble, dedicated, introverted, green thumb, proper, helpful, proactive, homemaker, the maiden

SHADOW: follower, demanding, irritable, neurotic, compliant, finicky, conservative, pessimistic, hypercritical, single-minded, disinterested, picky, high-strung, judgmental, defiant, anxious, ungrateful, weed-infested garden

Scene The Ocelot hides in the dense thickets as the daisies tickle her toes, intently watching as you approach her lair. Excited by the prospect of being seen, the Queen's heart pounds as she pants with anticipation. Shifting slightly, unable to get comfortable, the hairs down the ridge of her sleek back raise, ready to pounce at a moment's notice as she waits. You hear a strange sound coming from a small opening, and your stomach flutters as you lean in to take a closer look. Suddenly your gaze locks with the most-beautiful crystalline topaz eyes, which immediately narrow into slits. You feel her stare probing you, automatically raising your hands and freezing in place, fearing to make the slightest move. The Ocelot rewards this interaction with a hiss, causing the hairs on the back of your neck to stand at attention in warning.

Locked in this stalemate, you feel something probing at your consciousness as you hear soundless words form in your mind: "I am the Queen of Pentacles. You will address me as such. You have now entered my realm." You open your mouth to respond, but nothing escapes, so wisely you hold your tongue. Your eyes move upward to her crown, admiring the intricate design intertwined with flora pulsating with life. You are instantly drawn to the golden pentacle in the center of her headdress. Her melodic voice is telepathically heard again: "You're looking for answers. I will oblige with this: if people don't come into your life with the desire to love you, they have come with the intention to use you." This truth hits you right in the center of your chest, causing you to exhale the breath you didn't realize you were holding, squeezing your eyes shut, savoring the moment. Hand-over-heart nodding in reverence to the Queen, you smile as you turn away into the awaiting arms of your future.

Queen of Pentacles in Love She is a devoted partner who radiates nurturing and stability, providing comfort and security. Her love is grounded and abundant and blossoms like a well-tended garden. If single, this Queen is really picky and takes her time in finding the best suitable partner.

Queen of Pentacles in Career This Queen in career is management material, demonstrating responsibility and steadfastness. With exceptional focus and determination, she effortlessly achieves her goals. Taking pride in her workspace, she decorates it to reflect her personality, creating a nurturing and comfortable environment that feels just like home.

Queen of Pentacles in Wellness As a natural overthinker, this Queen reminds you to pay attention to the abdominal area and digestive system. As a worrier, she feels everything deeply, often exhibiting hypochondriac tendencies and excessive health concerns. To maintain balance, this Queen must keep her anxiety in check.

Queen of Pentacles in Finances This Queen confidently works her way up the corporate ladder or social ladder through marriage. It matters not which one, for she embraces the attitude that money is money regardless of its origin. This Queen works hard to accumulate wealth and raise her status while filling her coffers.

The Astrological Sign of the Queen of Pentacles Virgo (August 23–September 22)

Words of Wisdom from the Queen of Pentacles Nurture your dreams like a bountiful garden, for the Queen of Pentacles knows the alchemy of turning aspirations into gold.

Spirit Guide—Ocelot Cat The Ocelot comes striding into your life, bringing the gift of seeing things as they are. Her sleek, beautiful markings remind you that life does not run in a straight line; there will always be spots, patches, and paths. This intriguing exotic cat is exceptionally good at finding work-arounds for all of life's obstacles, promising to walk beside you when you've lost your way.

> *Success is getting what you want.*
> *Happiness is wanting what you get.*
> **Ingrid Bergman**

King of Pentacles

As King I come to show that
dedication brings success
Truthfully speaking, there's one thing
I must confess
The secret to my achievements
is knowing your worth
And taking your rightful place,
as borne by your birth

KEYWORDS & CONCEPTS

LIGHT: ambitious, accountable, disciplined, reliable, traditionalist, proactive, business savvy, steadfast, courteous, influential, conscientious, professional, trustworthy, resourceful, unfazed, leadership, structured, respectful

SHADOW: opportunist, irritable, self-critical, capitalist, nervousness, rigidity, financially controlling, reserved, seriousness, undisciplined, prudent, persistent, grumbling, mistrustful, perfectionist, cautious, know-it-all, unrelenting

Scene The Red Stag watches you intently as you cross the threshold. Entering into his realm, you notice him sizing you up from head to toe. Seated before you, he is a glorious beast with a crimson crown nestled in the center of his huge rack, proudly displaying his power and status of kingship. You feel a majestic aura surrounding him. As he levels his gaze upon you, it feels as though he's peering into the depths of your soul. Cocking his head to one side, he inquires, "What's brought you so far off your path?" You let out a heavy sigh and tell him, "I seem to have lost my way. But I saw the glow of this lantern and decided to follow the light, and it led me here." The Red Stag looks at you with a curious gleam in his eye and says, "I am the King of Pentacles; I've lived long enough to know when I see a lost soul." The words settle on you like a gloomy cloud on a rainy day. Shuffling your feet and lowering your eyes, you softly say, "How did you know?" The King continues speaking in a soothing tone with kindly words: "As you walk your path of solitude, you were clever to follow the light, since sometimes you have to travel the forgotten road to remember who you are." You feel a sense of peace engulf you, listening intently as he has more to say. "I guarantee that if you set your intention, work hard, and never give up, you'll receive unimaginable success. Handle rejection and naysayers with grace by paying them no heed, and never let anyone or anything stand in your way of achieving your goals." Rubbing the center of your chest, you felt that one.

Smiling with gratitude, you bow low, thanking the King for the sage advice. Slowly rising, now standing at full height, a surge of profound illumination washes over you. Waving goodbye, you turn away, finding the footpath. You lay your hand over your heart, reclaiming the seed within your soul. Feeling its radiant growth merge with your inner radiance, you smile as you shine enlightenment out into the world.

King of Pentacles in Love When this King loves, he loves hard. Once his trust is broken, it's irreparable, leaving no room for second chances. He is fair, thoughtful, and considerate as a partner, proud to provide for his partner. A true Renaissance man, he embodies a savviness when it comes to love and relationships.

King of Pentacles in Career The quintessential business man, the King of Pentacles possesses the ultimate entrepreneur spirit, achieving great success in everything he endeavors. This King typically finds himself in positions of financial authority within the organization, making a wonderful CFO and yet a generous practical boss.

King of Pentacles in Wellness The King of Pentacles advises tending to your knees, bones, and skin, keeping joints limber through gentle movements and stretching. Channel this King's determination to achieve health-and-wellness goals.

King of Pentacles in Finances This King excels in managing finances and spotting unique business opportunities while maintaining a keen eye on his accounts. He possesses a "money talks" attitude, valuing others with a similar status.

The Astrological Sign of the King of Pentacles Capricorn (December 22–January 19)

Words of Wisdom from the King of Pentacles The ancient soil beneath your feet cradles the hidden treasures of abundance. Tenderly cultivate the seeds of your soul and watch them flourish into a magnificent forest of prosperity and fulfillment.

Spirit Guide—Red Stag As King of both realms, his hooves are firmly grounded, while majestic antlers reach toward the spirit world. The eight points represent maturity, and with continuous growth comes the ability to annually shed what no longer serves him. The Red Stag invites you to go beyond your comfort zone, embarking on wonderful adventures and creating lasting memories that will carry on, long after you're gone. Embrace the wisdom of abundance and the power of determination as you nurture your spirit toward a prosperous path, leaving a great legacy behind.

Number one, cash is king . . . number two, communicate . . .
number three, buy or bury the competition.
Jack Welch

Spreads

Tarot spreads are like road maps, guiding you through the realm of possibilities. They provide insights by highlighting motives, shining the light on blind spots, and exploring probable outcomes. By engaging your intuition, you're focusing on the space in between the cards, revealing sacred wisdom there. Each spread has its unique design, arranging the cards to represent different aspects of your questions or situations.

Here are a few of my favorites:

THREE-CARD SPREADS

Lay out the cards horizontally 1, 2, 3 and use these examples of simple but powerful three-card spreads

The Eight of Tarot (the Strength card): strength, weakness, potential

The Wellspring: healing, forgiveness, release

Mourning Eternally: the grief, the acceptance, the healing light

The Mirror of Truth: the reflection, the shadow, the authentic self

The Door: the awakening, the unveiling, the transformation

Embracing Shadows: the darkness, the surrender, the awakening

Crossroads of Destiny: the choice, the path, the outcome

The Path of Purpose: the calling, the skills, the fulfillment

Soul's Embrace: the past connection, the present union, the future harmony

LOOKING FOR LOVE FIVE-CARD SPREAD

1. **Ethereal:** How can I attract love into my life?
2. **Intention:** What energy signature am I sending into the universe?
3. **Attraction:** Which of my qualities shine brightest to attract love into my life?
4. **Love:** How can I love myself more, so I have the capacity to love another?
5. **The Blind Spot:** What is hindering me from finding love?

PERSPECTIVE NINE-CARD SPREAD

1. **Energy at play:** What energies surround the situation?
2. **Unseen corners:** What am I missing or overlooking?
3. **Gaining distance:** What insights emerge when I step back?
4. **A higher view:** What wisdom is revealed from above?
5. **Shifting tides:** How is the situation dynamically evolving?
6. **Focal point:** What essential element demands my focus?
7. **Divine whispers:** What spiritual guidance is offered?
8. **Optimal path:** What course of action is most favorable?
9. **Emerging possibilities:** What outcome lies in the foreseeable horizon?

Through enchanted woods we wandered,
a Fool's journey intertwined
In The Westwood Tarot we met characters,
where ancient archetypes aligned
Heard whispers of sacred arcana;
together we danced among the trees
Until we meet again, my friend, in new worlds
and words of mysteries

Author Bios

Yasmeen Westwood is a self-taught photomanipulation artist living in Perthshire in Scotland. Her first deck—*The Tarot of Enchanted Dreams*—was released in December 2019. She was a finalist for her artwork, for the MPower, Mums in Business National Business Awards 2019. For *The Tarot of Enchanted Dreams*, she was runner-up in two categories of the International Tarot Foundation CARTA Awards 2019, for Best Illustrator of a Tarot Deck and Best Self-Published Tarot Deck, and she won the Bronze for Tarot Decks in the COVR awards in 2020. Her other decks include *Hummingbird Wisdom Oracle* (won Gold, Product of the Year, Industry Choice of the Year, and Peoples Choice of the Year and in the COVR 2022 Awards), *Tarot of the Enchanted Soul* (Gold Winner, COVR Awards 2023), *Angels of Healing & Hope* (Silver, COVR Awards 2023), and the recently released *Lenormand of Enchantment*. www.Enchantedsoulart.co.uk

Kalliope, named after the Muse of Epic Poetry, possesses an innate connection to magick and divination. Guided by ancestral wisdom, she delves into Tarot's symbolic secrets. Since 1986, she has wholeheartedly embraced its transformative power to profoundly heal and change lives. With over three decades of experience, Kalliope serves as a trusted earth guide offering soulful insights and guidance worldwide. Her mastery is beautifully showcased in her acclaimed book *Lenormand of Enchantment*. As a sought-after teacher and speaker, she generously shares her wisdom, guiding others on their soul's path. Residing by the tranquil lakeside in southern Ontario, Kalliope finds inspiration in the loving presence of her King of Swords, two beloved boys, and her faithful black cat, Spell. Visit her at www.musekalliope.com.